SELECTED POEMS

SELECTED POEMS

Michael Anania

ASPHODEL PRESS

MOYER BELL

WAKEFIELD, RHODE ISLAND AND LONDON

Published by Asphodel Press

Grateful acknowledgment is made to the following
publications in which some of the previously un-
collected poems in this book first appeared:
*Apalachee Quarterly, Illinois Review, Journal, Private,
Scripsi, Tri-Quarterly, Wire, Zeitung.*

"Pochades" was published in a Haybarn Editions
portfolio with lithographs by Ed Colker. "Touch-
ing the Ground" was written for and first pub-
lished by The Parliament of the World's
Religions.

The jacket art is a detail of *White Ford Overdrive* by
Ralph Goings. Permission is given by the artist
and O.K. Harris Works of Art, New York NY.

LIBRARY OF CONGRESS
CATALOGING-IN-PUBLICATION DATA

Anania, Michael, 1939–
  [Poems. Selections. 1994]
  Selected Poems / Michael Anania.
  1st ed.
    p. cm.
  ISBN 1–55921–113–X
  I. Title.
  PS3551.N25A6   1994
  811'.54—dc20   CIP

Printed in the United States of America.
Distributed in North America by Publishers
Group West, P.O. Box 8843, Emeryville, CA
94662, 800-788-3123 (in California 518-658-
3453).

for Joanne, from the start

CONTENTS

STOPS ALONG
THE WESTERN BANK
OF THE MISSOURI RIVER

Yes, we will gather at the river,
the beautiful, the beautiful river;
yes we will gather at the river,
the beautiful river of love.

When this problem has been thoroughly explored,
I am going to school myself so well in things
that, when I try to explain my problems,
I shall speak, not of self, but of geography.

—Pablo Neruda

A Journey

for Ted Mallory
(who died, December 1963)

I Grace Street

Just north of Clark Street
Grace Street, disheveled,
without the regimen of red brick,
the houses, grey of old wood
stripped of paint above
the tilted, broken walks,
cracked by the roots of elms
that hang over the walks,
break open retaining walls,
that spread green over the grey,
light green after the torn husks
sift into the broken walls
and down to the earth beneath
the canted, cracked sidewalks.
Grace Street due east
across thoroughfares,
level to the Boulevard,
past a gutted store
with a drawn coonskin
drying on the grey wall,
level to the brewery
then down to the yards,
to the open sewer that
swills into the river.

II Crosstown Transit

How did we move across the city
along the baseline of August?
Swaying in a dusty streetcar—
by the recitation of streets
from Grace Street south,
by counting hills, hollows,
by marking the familiar buildings,
counting store-front signs.
How far now in the mad dream?
Cecil's Barber Shop, Mason Street,
Rees Street across the playground
west, up its short hill four blocks
past my grandfather's two small houses.
We know the old black man asleep,
bobbing like a fish in the slow river,
sprawled over the yellow wicker seat;
Crosstown knows Mr. King's face,
deep brown skin stretched
over black bones,
the deep sound of his jostled sleep,
our faces, white and black.

III Dead August

Dead August, I remember
the hard, cracked earth,
the street-sides full of dust.
The slow river runs scum
streamers from sewers,
hangs about bridge pilings,
seems almost still;
an old black fisherman
wrinkles the shadows of a doorway,
dreams of bullheads, long horns.
Clark Street at the silent turning
of shadows in the dust of August,
a passing car rearranges the atmosphere
raising a cloud of fine curb dust,
a carp breaks water in a swirl of scum
then slips back into the ages of mud
as the dust sifts through sunlight
into heavy air.

IV Afterthoughts

The open land,
Indians on horseback,
round hills rising
from the still dark river,
the horses dragging sleds,
women walking over open land,
behind the horses, bronze stragglers.
At the flats where the river bends
a party of white men,
a dark woman standing apart
looking to round hills—
Afterthoughts.   First,

the city is dust,
rain hard on the dust,
snow and heavy, white smoke-clouds,
dead of summer, dead of winter.
We move through intersections
capable of history.
Birdwoman, bronze lady of the river,
figurehead of keelboats,
steel lady of bridges,
we pass in the dead of August.

Missouri Among Rivers

*"I have heard that nothing is of itself;
must I, therefore, speak of dependencies?"*

The river I commend to you so often,
brown with mud, yellow in sunlight,
moves between green hills in the west,
you know from sea songs
is the opening of the land.

Wind River plummets through
its own ferrous gorge,
makes a dance figure of the seasons,
of wind and rain, an attitude of time;
fallen boulders, the rapids
render the fall, the arc to the crest
played out, the violent picturesque.

I will not be led by complications of grandeur;
there is more to learn from the dull Platte,
meager, cutting streams through sand bars,
trees gathered about its banks,
the prairies behind them.

Let us consider the migration of trees,
the birch seeds that drifted down
from the forests of Minnesota,
how they came upstream with the Platte.

The trees are green, the prairies green with corn;
the waters of the Platte enter the brown river
in no great ecstacy.
Bluff crests in Fontenelle are quiet,
give no emblem's figured name.

Shear Face

This bluff face, brown and yellow clay,
is called Devil's Slide, sometimes Suicide Hill.
There, just below the cliff's edge,
where elm roots fork out into open air,
young men dig caves for love
a hundred feet above
the river road, the silt flats.
Take the slide, top to bottom,
in a cardboard box. Be a legend
across the lined clay face,
over bent shrub trees.
In the evening the lovers lead their girls
to the top, over the edge to their dark caves,
and if they need to wait a bit,
they look out over the river to hills in Iowa,
to green and red river lights
and the lights of Mormon Bridge.
Take count of what they say,
lovers who have swung by elm roots
above the river, through the hot summer,
cutting trails, digging into hard wet earth.
We come after, on Sunday morning
to the top in a Plymouth tudor,
and I notice how the ground fog
slides down channeled bluffs,
and you say it's beautiful.

Of The River Itself

This is my advice to foreigners:
call it simply—*the river;*
never say old muddy
or even Missouri,
and except when it is necessary
ignore the fact that it moves.
It is *the river,* a singular,
stationary figure of division.
Do not allow the pre-Socratic
to enter your mind except
when thinking of clear water trout
streams in north central Wyoming.
The river is a variety of land,
a kind of dark sea or great bay,
sea of greater ocean.
At times I find it good discipline
to think of it as a tree
rooted in the delta,
a snake on its topmost western branch.
These hills are not containers;
they give no vantage but that
looking out is an act of transit.
We are not confused,
we do not lose our place.

Elmwood

Decay is brilliance.

The walk curves downward
out of congested sunlight
into light divided by mottled elms—
sunlight separated into colors
above the yellowing grass.

It is a watershed,
this small valley,
the creek in the hollow
now clotted with leaves
dissipates into storm sewers
and enters the river
mingled with refuse.

October elmwood in bright sunlight—
an organ aging and diseased,
the cornea crusted with red and yellow
dead and dying leaves,
the retina, you and I
in useless poise at the center—
esto nobis, the glutted stream.
We are stream, river, gulf and sea
in an eye of elmwood
at the fission of light.

Arbor Lodge

Make it a monument:
where the highway
bends past the birches,
the cabin with slotted gunports,
before the shaded gate
fix a new stone marker,
an emblem freely carved.
In the great house
mark the chair where
Bryan sat after dinner,
wing-backed before
the bellied windows,
looking eastward wearily
toward the end of his new world.
Plains blue stem grass,
delicate and discrete,
flutters at the roadside,
extinct except at the roadside,
where fluted seeds drawn out
by a rush of vehicles
scatter across the pavement
and are planted at the roadside.

Mandan

This is my own wilderness
beginning with my fingertips,
cascade tree stubble to silt;
at my right hand, Fontenelle,
mule fawn in green dark,
soft dapple of touch
by sunlight through
leaves brown and green.
It is forest here
with the plains
opening at my back—
the Platte to Northfork,
Chimney Rock and Courthouse Rock.
Mandan in memory of the dead—
deer rustle among dead leaves
and slip elms—memorial of
nine villages to the north
that were clustered about
the head-waters of the river's
southward flow, a turn
bending down to Fontenelle,
the soft soil that holds
against generations of rainwater
the dark stains of their covered fires.

The Square: Bum's Park

Smells of urine,
cheap cologne,
Tiger Rose and sour milk
hang in the staircase—
the Chicago Hotel
the elite of Omaha
overlooking beautiful
Jefferson Square.
Old men on benches
under trees
nod in silence
sleep
dripping black
snuff spittle from
the corners of their
lined mouths, sleep.
Hot August morning—
a game of tag weaves
through the trees
past the water faucet
into the dry fountain,
spins to rest
like a swirl of dust
on a windless day.
This was the hallowed ground
that Cowboy Jim
went to bat for,
one of four squares

given at corporation
for public use.
He said it was essential,
hung with red lights,
a center of life.
They wore sheets,
burned a cross,
hung the black boy
from a telegraph pole.
It was all planned to cause
unrest so they could say
Cowboy Jim was right
keep all the evil in one place;
there's no such thing as reform.

The Park Above All Others
Called, Riverview

for David Bahr

A bust of Schiller on a hillside
faces east, looks like a Medici.
It could all be so right,
remembering the glorious songs,
the plainness of Der Handschuh,
lions and tigers lying down together;
Lorenzo and Alberti met on Sundays
in the Daphnis hills north of Florence,
practiced the vernacular,
made jokes of the scholars;
Johannes studied alchemy in Venice,
and some rude German poled through
the reflection of Oldenburg Cathedral;
Monet waited to be French.
From the Schiller hill in Riverview
the park lagoon looks green and deep brown,
green moss on the stone water wall.
From the far side of the lagoon
the green lawn rises to a high hill;
heavy with trees, it blocks the river view.
If you stand tiptoe on the seashore,
climb the log tower on Race Point Road,
the sea hills too high for a view of the Azores.
Boys with their Polish grandmother
are intent on bubbles rising,
lower gum foil
to tempt a hidden crayfish.

The old woman adjusts her shawl,
mimics green hills, Poland
and the very year of my birth;
like crayfish to Warsaw,
the roads are long and straight
lined with beech trees,
and the dust rises like bubbles.
From the Pathé version remember
the workings of the Green Plan,
the exfoliation of steel.
How does it matter,
this view of the park by the river?
Not as a start, that is confusion.
It is the going about place
where we act out what we know;
it is saying straight out—
it is the recurrent dream
demanding the voice that speaks through.

VALEETA

Once more
and then
goodnight
to the sailor
Valeeta
across the plaza
in red velveteen
glitter on her shoes
early birds catch
early light.
It is good–
morning Valeeta
not goodnight.

NIGHTS AT THE BON TON

Good old red and blue
bubbles up and down your face,
serenade the paper moon
pal-o-mine, no disgrace
when love was ready
your sweetheart ran away;
a nickle a song, play
play on forever,
dance the twirling
crepe-paper, swing and sway
Blue Baron, like the ballroom,
dancing among needles of turning lights,
diamonds and pearls at the sweat rings shine.

TO MYSELF AND FOR AUGUST 5, 1964

I have a new tie from France
  a recollection of dance
(sometimes I'm clumsy).
Now that I'm too old to be the son
  you wish you'd had,
how do you all dream of me
  behind your drawn shades
in the blue light of television.
Have I become a lover
  not a passing son,
each day less of myself
  more a Lash LaRue—
dandy with a holdout,
  a trickster,
like Jesse, my father,
  master of the cull-shuffle.
Am I a songster or a dealer?

A STRATAGEM

(after Ehrich Weiss)

I

Geography matters.
It is the plan,
the arrangement of things
that confuses our enemies,
the difference between what
they expect and what they get;
as simple as bobbing for apples
becomes difficult, deception is
an achievement in ordering the obvious.

II

Let us make a song
for our confusion:
Call it "Red Skies over Gary"
or "Red Skies in the Sunset"
or "Red Skies and the Open Hearth."

   Red Skies over Gary,
   you are my sunset,
   my only home.

Let us make ourselves invisible,
not make songs, or even
disappear suddenly from
the sidewalks of Calumet.

III

Cobalt and carborundum
are refinements of the art.

So it's true, you held
the razor in your teeth,
or was it pure magic,
a miracle of place?
One makes for workability,
the other for hardness,
and chromium bright,
the stainless achievement.

IV

I came from Calumet to Gary,
and it was early evening;
south of the mills, poppy fields
toxic red above the car lots,
have a Coke on Texaco
'til the mercury arcs devour us
and it is purple night.

COMPLAINT

Why must you sleep like that
curled up and turned away,
your limbs indistinguishable,
the blanket drawn up over
your mouth like a fan,
like a fan hiding a smile.

DRIFTS

Or else were this a savage spectacle.

Dissonant, drawn out,
interposed by a flat
flute song, ancient
melody, at least,
the snow, furled out
between bare trees,
lunar—played by
the drone of snow-
tires, untuned:
the electric organ plays
the radio plays
the wind plays
all songs.

It is the measure
of nothing.
"In the beauty of the lilies
Christ was born across the street."
Of snow born white, caught
on an imperfection of asphalt,
it grows, increases,
drifts to shape and form.

Sic transit savior
at the bypass,
at this point,
the present chaos
of music, shapeless,
the holy fountain,

Siloa out of the
black pothole,
reversion across
the street I track
with chaotic song.

SONGS FROM AN INSTITUTION #1

Wreck of a pearl-diver, old bastard
gone to bad wine, sterno and koolade
came home in '45 with tatoos for
mother and Rosemarie, the jungle rot
goes sour every summer or in the spring
when the rain stands out in pools.

His wife left him in a year,
said she couldn't stand the smell
or even the look, it looks like leprosy;
the mud and the water, he says,
got inside me with the blood or
deep down where it used to be.

SONGS FROM AN INSTITUTION #2

Lovejoy,
my heart goes out to
the French girl on
the mountain. Oh
Larson, Larson
where are you now?
did I leave you
with your guts out
or did you turn,
in the end, on me,
why won't you tell
is it that you too
love the French girl
high on the mountain?

SONGS FROM AN INSTITUTION #3

I was at Iwo
beneath the bronzed men,
there where it cuts off to the base
held my ground against a thousand;
they hogged all the glory,
puked at the groans of heroes,
my own cries; the whole world
cheers and cries for me.
I am a soldier, a movie,
imitation of my celluloid
march through the
forests and marshes of Leyte,
bearded with a cigarette
slouched against a tree
forceful, unconcerned.
She fell for me right off
because I spoke Chinese,
took her figured skirt off
and did a deadly dance.

A SECOND-HAND ELEGY

for Douglas Dickey, Pfc. U.S.M.C.

"How can I be bitter?"
the fence-rows rolling with the land;
the last full measure of Ohio
measured by fence-rows compressing,
though parallel above receding hills,
the mixed hues of damp Spring greenery.

"I never knew him to be angry or afraid."
that is, assured of a providence
moving within the accidental turnings
of his life, he moved with certainty
among the farmyard's familiar disorders
and occasionally outward toward Dayton.

"He glanced for an instant at his friends—
    for only an instant—and then he jumped."
riding through Dayton on Saturday night
making the rounds, block by block,
the car radio marking time—
Downtown   Downtown—
the evening blush of neon blooming.
into damp city air, the blue
clarity of mercury-lamp arcades;
four of them slouched in a Chevrolet
exhaust the evening, waiting for something to happen.

Note: In April of 1968 Douglas Dickey was awarded the Congressional Medal of Honor posthumously for throwing himself on a hand grenade during an engagement with the enemy in Viet Nam.

LINES FOR GRACE SLICK

I

hit was a ladie
carried a knife,
as they say, on
or about her person;

sidewalks and alley-
ways, unlit entrances,
she knew and moved
among them with grace

wythouten spotte
the blade she flashed,
looking for the least
flaw of light along

the edge, up to its
quick-sprung hilt,
the love they spoke,
began and ended with

II

swich wordes and gentilesse
swinging the telephone
by the cord, caught him
just above the ear

the cone of the mouth-
piece spinning away,
round shaft cracked in
two, dial-tone sustained

na trauayle there
ready to alter by
saying, touching;
pieces fall like china,

noises that succeed
his fall, dull sound
of collapsed clothing;
she had no refrain

OCTOBER TRIPTYCH

for Jo and Harry Hayford

It begins with
lake-gulls, white and silent,
on pilings that flank a lake
faceted with ripples, windlessly
lapping pillars, soft with wet-rot
and the horizon, vague
in spite of sun breaks through
cloud cover miles out, patching
with shining plaques, dull grey water

and moves to trees, nearly bare,
a network of bruised limbs
that resurface this dark sky—
glaze and texture of Bosch—
with occasional bright red,
red of maple and sumac,
opening sinfully where
wet with morning, the branches cross

then swings out finally to an afternoon
at edgewater with feeding gulls
adrift, buoying white in the dark,
soft stuff of an autumn michigan.

NOVEMBER REQUIEM TO OURSELVES

Erie

    where slate planes
        out into the lake

   the sand
       black with slate fragments

   the water
       black above black slate

    on the dunes
   the slate faces windward
              to the lake

  black extrusions
   at the head of the land

          At Erie we walked
          picked through pebbles
          broke the delicate slate
          between our fingers
          talked about summer

     the bright sun

   the wind, the feathered squalls
      black on black

organic, growing
    changing shapes
    across the dance
        of the inevitable rollers

    late leaves twist
        over the sand
            through the pebbles
      sandstone, quartz
        discolored, ferrous

and burnt-out, broken
        dismembered
an old fire
    was autumn.

FOR EZRA POUND, OLD

She turned her head away, but it was plain
that she was greatly moved and excited.
W. C. Williams, Autobiography

Of a new vintage proffered,
now an age of fashioning:
past fifty years by force of mallet,
a flat cup for dry leaves.

Autumn.
The wind is cold in the new season
and she is silent, waiting
amid broad leaves on a flat cup,
a cold wind across dry leaves.

She is a woman of seasons offering change,
wine stains in lined silver, dull-eyed,
yet she is the agent of her own passing:
a spirit among dry leaves, a cold wind.

There is clemency this season;
we have counted in the harvest
and such prayers follow to watch
in new light the graving hand.

DEMI-ODE: BINOMIAL QUANTITIES

One adds or subtracts
(either/or); put it together,

then, the gold on itself
multiplied, as, later,

the water itself, plus
the two together, gold and water,

water over the gold—as in
a salver, a cup, rain across

a golden dome or rain aslant
in slanting light—however

arranged is twice the quantity,
or halved: "Behold the gold, this lyre,"

threads of light, watersong,
and there the dance, quenching fire.

THE FALL

I

Sunday in the snow
moving like an old man
I corner, slip and fall
with my hands out
twist my head to meet
the world I fall into—
present, precise to the moment
concrete, stinging, exact.
    The snow trees
feathered out with wind
across the damaged road
way, Route 20, through
township, east and west:
points of my life drawn
out along the thin, bending
highway—dead dog in Iowa,
the bridge at Clinton
arched like a scimitar
across the brown dream river;
Mississippi, Mohawk,
Niagara, Missouri,
did I dream you into
the world, as far off
as you now seem,
beaded out, lost to distance
by the fractured road.

II

The snow trees are luminous,
the frosted globes, archaic
by the neon signs, come on
like a flash. Mid-fall,
the fountain fills with snow;
I beat my arms in the air
like a cartoon cat finding
that my ladder is gone,
or do I remember, falling,
the girl in green
nightclothes lost on the highway,
the girl with the red eyes,
brown hair, green nylon
forced between her legs
by the base December wind,
screaming, help, screaming
with her fingers, red-tipped
in her blowing, brown hair,
or an unhinged door on the prairie,
or old newspapers across a lot
fluttering, tearing on a cyclone
fence. The lights go on and I
fall hands first in the snow.

III

My world goes out,
dream, distance, picture
ice on the river, I know,
gone to distance, broken
in the inevitable present.
I am incapable of the present
fall, while at koolade
cocktail parties no one
gasps, stops for a moment.
It must be reconstructed;
I can not find the beauty,
can not stop it at the
point of impact, can not
make the vision, what I see,
go on from beginning to end,
can not keep it going:
the clouds move, grey,
around the blurred moon,
the snow fills the streetlights,
the highway breaks to pieces
like Mr. Ripley's glass snake
because I touch it;
it will not rearrange itself.
In the lighted window worsted,
in the sky the red neon scrawl,
Pepsi Cola—Drink Light,

I drink light, bathe in light,
fall into my broken world.
It is the inevitable order
that destroys, the necessity
of falling, river to river
shore to shore,
instinctively outstretched
hands to the waiting ground.
Those are my hands breaking.
dream of my hand moving
with my eye, eye following
my hand from the word to the place.
Seeing breaks the storewindows;
the streetlights and neon are
falling together in the snow.

THE TEMPER

I think of you all
behind the steamed mirror
and I make a worthy face,
stern and unyielding,
to match your faces
on the photo-plate.
I am poseur,
what those brass eyes begat,
poet,
I see you in the frosted glass.

It is something to covet—
what my father said on the real McCoy,
the gesture and all of
holding the revolver in his hand,
tapping the butt on the table,
saying, that is solid,
more than this table, solid,
tempered blue sheen thunk
reflected on the table top,
snubnosed, hammerless real McCoy.
It is no less obvious for the tree,
the stone, Rabenstein (Valentin, useless fool,
spare us your bravura, leave us to ourselves).
It is not only a confusion after death
that the steam gathers into droplets
that run through us; we are no barrier
to the gathering in, changes in the weather.

Now we dream of absolute decline as jest;
it is the trail it leaves that we know,
martial of ending, begin with saying, our breath.

We remember and it is not enough, not nearly.
I say this as I am seen by men who broke the stone,
players in the pageant of Europe, and carried the callouses,
steerage in striped pants, to this river, my face in the glass.

DOCUMENT

Ellis Island and the confusion
over my grandfather's name
and my step-grandfather's name,
the Dutch barony called to question,
the transfer of the titled lands,
the lost stewardship, a new name.
This was the proof of the division
of Frank and Franz: the new world,
romance of the wanderer, stance—
Dakotas, Winter '08 to Summer '10,
Puget Sound, Winter '11 to Winter '13,
Alberta, Yukon Terr., Alaska,
Dakotas, Indian Terr., '14 to '22,
Nebraska Homestead, '23 to '25,
corner section township, '26.
When he died, F _____ said,
we remain divided at my ending
among blueberries, thistle,
dark to the world, Augenbaum;
polish me off like my father,
I die of pallor, faint green,
yellow. I am from the mountain,
speak *platt*. Generations of pawns
bring now an end to my name.
F _____ , of the oceans, plains,
mountains rivers west said,
I am he that

by this river, the opening plain,
said of the dust gathered about my feet,
this earth, my open hand and from it
to the farthest of my labors,
from home to home, end at beginning;
I remember the lowlands, the flowers,
full colors, mellifluous, I flow,
to goldenrod and sunflower,
flower of my hands, color of dust.
So the elegy of one, most western,
most free of the moving earth, death
of Europe for the other, the last words,
what was said, remembered of confusion,
hope of change was given in explanation.

AVANT COURIER

for Durrett Wagner

It is indeed a grand consent, or, rather, concert of forces—
the human energy or toil, the vital seed, and the polished
raindrop that never fails to fall in answer to the imploring
power or prayer of labor.
—Charles Dana Wilbur (1881)

How the dust gathered in drifts,
fence-high, barn-high,
sifted upward into unfinished eaves;
windowsills and doorsills
stuffed with rags, table linen,
pillow cases with hand-stitched flowers
clotted with mud, pried
out with knives and forks,
resoaked in mud-slaked water pails.

It held them that year
and the next—the working paths
through the barnyard strung with rope,
so that hand over hand they could
pull their way back through the thickened air,
the sun buried in the sky,
each furrow of the parceled land
spilling its seed into the choked wind.

A tinker named Anderson set out
from Coleridge, his tools secured

in oil-cloth, his mare's eyes bound
and was buried alive when his wagon
was mired in a cleft of dust,
that crossed the road like a snow curl,
arched over on the lea side, the print
of the wagon's clutter shadowed out
in irregularities of after-drift,
as though the crumpled line of his dying
had been shaken out like a thread
of loose flax, the strands breaking
into the distance, by cause alone
a measure of an obliterated shape.

MEMORIAL DAY

It is easily forgotten, year to
year, exactly where the plot is,
though the place is entirely familiar—
a willow tree by a curving roadway
sweeping black asphalt with tender leaves;

damp grass strewn with flower boxes,
canvas chairs, darkskinned old ladies
circling in draped black crepe family stones,
fingers cramped red at the knuckles, discolored
nails, fresh soil for new plants, old rosaries;

such fingers kneading the damp earth gently down
on new roots, black humus caught in grey hair
brushed back, and the single waterfaucet,
birdlike upon its grey pipe stem,
a stream opening at its foot.

We know the stories that are told,
by starts and stops, by bent men at strange joy
regarding the precise enactments of their own
gesturing. And among the women there will be
a naming of families, a counting off, an ordering.

The morning may be brilliant; the season
is one of brilliances—sunlight through
the fountained willow behind us, its splayed
shadow spreading westward, our shadows westward,
irregular across damp grass, the close-set stones.

It may be that since our walk there is faltering,
moving in careful steps around snow-on-the-mountain,
bluebells and zebragrass toward that place
between the willow and the waterfaucet, the way
is lost, that we have no practiced step there,
and walking, our own sway and balance, fails us.

A WAR STORY

(At this date exact order is impossible.)

The old women in black crepe, lights out,
pressed wrinkled hands on the table;
I was in the corner of the dark room
                    waiting.

        Consumed in fire completely—
        my Uncle Frank saw it happen
        and said five years afterwards
        that the noise was unbearable;
        the shells make long, sharp screams,
        fill the air with water and wet sand.
        Like jellied fire, he said,
        opening from a great balloon,
        and he was immersed in fire.
        Nothing could be done.

It was an old table, pressed paper on wooden legs,
with flowers, roses, it seems now, pink and red.
I conceived of my part as holding order of objects
against the darkness, thick with hung sausage and aging
                    cheese.

        Table, with roses, pink and red,
        where is my son Antonio Joseph?

The studio couch escapes me;
if I can divide the nostrils,
smell all the garlic and cheese
with the left, say, and save the other
for breathing—I can't open my mouth—
it is possible to hold my place.

who was beautiful in white
and loved saints' stories.
Holy Mother understand me
with roses, pink and red,
I come for my son Antonio Joseph.

(Here the public account does service:
the news came and women wailed.)

Sensation is the impediment to design:
remember this—that was all on Rees Street
which runs East and West exactly
doesn't intersect the North-South transit
missing by one block, the playground;
extended it would span the earth,
to this the table was parallel,
or rather, being square on any side,
either parallel or perpendicular.

The studio couch was old and rounded,
did not admit of design, escaped me,

and the old women changed faces
as they changed seats around the table
and the pink and red roses tossed their
petals in the still, heavy air;
there was never a smell of roses
although she said:

    These roses of sweet fragrance
    I bring in offering for my son,
    have mercy on one who loves you.

        This is a shrapnel from
        the first world war
        and will serve to make the point;
        this smooth side is the machined
        outer facing of the shell;
        this peak, the sharp edges
        and the long point show
        how it was torn to pieces,
        how it flew through the air.
        I show you now the old wounds
        in my stomach, my neck and
        my thigh as examples of pain.

Epode

I can say only that this comes back from seeing yesterday
    the bright sun, bright blue sky in Winter
and it is entirely possible that if it were overcast and drear
    important parts, the color of the flowers,
the beginning, I'm sure, would be very different indeed, it is
    hard to say whether it is worth the thought.

In any case whatever lament there is to it comes from fact
    or should I admit order of fact
which was entirely accidental, if anything, uncontrollable
    considering the kind of day it was,
cold with no wind and the snow's blind sparks up from
                                 everywhere
    except where the wind had forced it deep into the trees.

And what Maud said about tornadoes has nothing to do with
    it because she was always such a liar
and what my grandfather said is of no interest except that
    women are not to be trusted
and what was not said, the blank spaces, go without saying
    and, as they say, speak for themselves.

DIVERSIONS UPON AN OLD REFRAIN

One, the pebble
gathering in several places,
conversations, mere talk,
arrangements of objects,
or else, excursions, planned
outings to historic places;
after the first turn, the second;
before the retrospective supposition
and the sideways glance, halfsteps
and falterings scrape between buildings

One, the pebble
Suffering a lapse of memory
how the fog yields up a place,
solace; she holds my hand
beneath the cottage fretwork,
speaks as slow music, half heard;
later, in the garden, muttering
into sleep, as though of . . .

One, the pebble
as in the clinic, waiting for vaccination
with Susan Marsh, her fingers knotting
the hem of her dress; one minute past,
Mrs. Danielson screaming, "My liver,
I've lost my liver, I tell you doctor
I've lost my liver"; waiting the next
ruffle of the cards to stir a slouched

figure out of the knave of benches
down the aisle to the swinging gate

   One, the pebble
hand without fingernails,
fingertips calloused over;
"What do you do?" a hand
of stubbed fingers pressed
against your face; "skinner"
he said, one hand for the knife,
the other tearing without nails
at the greased edge of the hide,
thumb hooked to the first finger

   One, the pebble
slipped down the plaza stairs,
shouting "rape" to her husband,
five minutes back from Greenland,
her gentlemen callers' Chevrolet
vanished up the alley trailing smoke;
policemen, taking notes, scuff
about the stoop; the husband stands
before his door holding a dufflebag;
you cannot see his face; light from
the doorway converts him into shadows

   One, the pebble
in the walkway past the icehouse,
urine and broken bottles, winos
hunched in against wind, rain,
snow, the sunlight, the spotlight;
one blocks the way, palms pressed

53

to opposing walls, demanding,
"Know your bible, sonny, the oldest
man in the bible died before his father,
get it? get it? know your bible"—
the passage opening where water
fountains all day behind grey slats,
angled upward, that show only the spray

   One, the pebble
hands burning in the cinder path
behind Ratner's dump, tireless
wheels buried among rusted cans;
saw them push through stiff weeds,
heard the car door squeak open;
guess each breath taken, practice,
in the dark grit, quick hands moving;
sniff down through a Packard's
opened canvas roof—nothing but
the must of grease and mildew

   One, the pebble
lady of the Tudor cottage, polite,
my welfare her only real concern,
shifts the shadows on the garden wall,
bringing tea and cakes, one minute past,
distinguishing flowers that close
at sunset from those that bloom
until they fall, brown-edged, petal
by petal to the close-cut grass;
"ask me no questions and I'll tell you"

One, the pebble
a movie, a novel, misremembered;
the amnesiac, a soldier, myself
wandering narrow English streets;
to the bobby on the corner,
thank you, yes, I'm alright now,
thank you, to the lady in the garden
as the past edges back, remembering

One, the pebble
lady, the thread of the movie gathers
you back into the cottage, your garden
of mixed flowers is drawn in around you
like a needle-work coverlet, uncovering
a garden of weeds and gutted cars,
where a pennant of latex hangs from a gearshift,
where someone named Sally walks with one
and is met by many; forty-five in all
mount the shredded moleshair cushion

One, the pebble
the cinder, the square of glass
that flakes off shattered *Safte-Seal,*
the night's progress, one plus one,
returning against a poet drowsing,
forgetful as a soldier from some
implicit war or a dreamer intent on loss

One, the pebble

THE RIVERSONGS
OF ARION, I-X

*The Rule is one, like itself accompanied with stability and rest;
if once we go astray from that, there is neither end nor quiet in
error, but restlessness and emptiness.*

—Thomas Hooker (1659)

This evening Guthrege Cought a White Catfish . . .
tale much like that of a Dolfin.

Journals of Lewis and Clark
(July 24, 1804)

I

Adrift on an oil-drum raft
I have traveled this river south
past packinghouse spills

with split-bellied watermelons
and castaway chicken heads.
I have seen catfish and bullheads

feed among the scum that eddies
beneath eroded silt shoals
and heard the silver tankers

taxi across crestfallen bluffs
at the fenced bend above the Platte's
mouth and caught, now, at midstream

on a rusted snare of dredge cable
with the slow brown water curling
dark foam against barrel heads,

my fingers track the grain of dry plank,
measuring the dull cadence of bare
feet over a worn poler's tread.

II

The river's wavelets,
thick with sewage, move,
it seems, upstream against

final deposit in some
widening delta. Illusive.
It is the rush beneath

speeding as the deep
channel bends; the surface
moving more slowly, inertial,

is curled back and downward.
So, when catfish feed
in quick channel waters,

they move upstream, angling
into the surface just as
the curling wave is pulled

back. Rivermen call this
the catfish dance because
from the banks they seem

stationary, bobbing up
and down in the dark foam.
Marquette feared the thud

of their bodies against
his canoe; treacherous,
the roiling brown waters,

Pekitanoui, route to
the vermillion sea, with
large branches, whole trees
adrift, floating islands,
the channel blue, called
ponderosa. Goodrich's white?

a common channel cat, up to
four feet, *punctatus*. I wait.
White Catfish Camp—that stretch

of silt, as good as any, any
song, river, now, like furrowed
loam, dendrite bluffs. They leap.

III ("the always restless, always moving on")

Some years before set
forth by raft across
the oil-slick sludge
of Angel Lake, SE
off Locust Street
toward Paxton-Vierling
and the U.P. Shops.

    He called himself The Kid,
    said: Like The Kid don't
    take no shit from nobody.
    Said: Like don't nobody
    fuck with The Kid.

The print of black water
along his arm, each pore
webbed with it, and washed
up over the packing-crate lid,
coming closer each time
he moved—THIS SIDE UP.
Locust Street viaduct behind
him, the freightyard, rail-
head pennies spread like leaves;
to the left, the drive-in movie
angling east; beam crane dead
ahead; windward, the city,
odors of cattle across steel.

The cool he put on
each morning, uneasy,
adjusted all day,
his arduous slouch,
flared cuffs, hair
oiled and arched back.

Somewhat confused, the surface
so much like creosote on wood,
and the evening closing down.
It was not what he had imagined,
night along the cinder shore,
hardly angelic, not a lake at all,
and the movie slivering its wedge
of light against tarnished silver,
his line of sight down the edge
of it—indistinguishable bright
objects, Monument Valley, perhaps,
thin strands of horses spilling
toward him like kelp in the crests
of long, persistent waves—the West,
Terminus, repeated everywhere, light
of the Rockies jostled with these
shadows, "never to be thrown down."

It was in Lincoln County,
the Lincoln County Wars, he
carved his name; in Texas
against carpetbaggers, home-
stead plundered, fiancé

promised to a storekeeper;
in Abilene against Hickok;
greased lightning; Vera Cruz,
that sunny afternoon, a smile;
"two sixes to beat," aces and eights
with his back to the door.

The sun hovers, cloudless sky,
town caught in its shadows,
a mother sweeps her child
away, curtains twitch; unseen
eyes, horseflesh ripples;
thin fingers that dealt smart
faro, cigar cupped in his hand;
it went to his lips, a shade slow,
the other, and fell for a border roll.

"I got no quarrel with you, Kid,"

so pulled her up into the saddle
behind him and rode away. How
sudden that sunset, saguaros.

Nowhere to go, riversump among refuse,
and under a ridge of pebbled glass—
skylights sooted dark as shale—
the Shops' nightsong, Union Pacific
hammered out "its dead indifference."

Dumbass, he said, skidding home,
loose heel-cleat scything his ankle.

IV

Dark-skinned with black hair
drawn tightly back, looking
northward through clay-ribbed
bluffs, she stood, I think,
ahead of the polers
in the keelboat's blunt
wet prow with a Yankee
helmsman facing her back,

and the wind, westerly—
out of my own childhood
and that unbroken prairie
where the Pawnee moved
like dust—shook the chewed
fringes of her buckskin dress.

". . . these barbary coasts . . ."

Stiff chokecherry thickets,
quick with sparrows, high
grasses where gray slag cuts
back to rain slides of yellow clay.
The same shores—or not? In time
the river sidewinds its banks.
Never the same soil; here, marks
of the land's uneven flow.

All fancy. She did not pass here,
met them half-a-year north,
already with child—Baptiste,
called Pomp, for Pompey—
with Lewis attending his birth,

> ". . . having the rattle of a snake by me I give it to
> him and he administered two rings of it to the
> woman broken in small pieces with the fingers and
> added to a small quantity of water. . . ."

yet the fringes, like pinfeathers,
her flight, the dream of home,
brown water opening twin petals
at her feet. The movie, that orange
novel, shapes of the river—mud slake
where she stands at some distance.
The campsite ebbs, now returns
like a wave. The treeline pitches
toward me, and there, a chokecherry
springs to a river tern's reach.

Before the empty plains,
spread like flat water
shoaling toward sand hills,
the first slopes, unarable,
of the dividing mountains,
the city squats above the river,
as an Indian woman at her

day's work might squat—
oblivious to the land behind her,
her hands full of the land—
red corn, dried meats, new skins.

At Rulo, Oto, Ponca, and Pawnee
camp on flats between bluff falls,
move west each morning in open trucks
to get a year's beet sugar in.

V (as Meriwether Lewis)

    Which river is this
    the first or the last?

fog like the old South
rising off slow water,
enclosing swamps

    Is that a waterthrush
    or falling water muted?

without channel markers
we often ran aground,
and it was impossible to
know whether we were lost
until a stream ran out
or we found a landmark,
Great Falls

    the deceptive waterthrush
    imitating falling water

each night I read my Journals
like a novel, seeking some
inevitability of plot, a hint
of form pointing toward an end

Am I remembering or acting again,
rounding out my own last scene
with a playwright's feel for disorder?

the cabin is filled with smoke,
like a Mandan lodge in winter,
women in the corners working skins,
young men striking flint on flint,
a man of words muttering to children
in the shadows past the firelight,
the brotherhood of wars turning
their faces to the banked fire:
floors of plank, a single table
like a keelboat, but smelling
of tallow, spilt ale, Virginia tobacco,
white smoke lit by the hearth fire,
a roadhouse lost in a river fog

    tavern odors and the far-off
    drip of water, thin as birdsong;
    the swampbird singing of water
    as the great waters quickly fall;
    fog touched with a hint of
    Cyprus standing in still water
    and spruce wet with mountain rain

there is a bend in thought
as treacherous as a river's bend
forked at the farthest side;

I have forgotten its meaning,
the lesson it holds for the sailor,
devout in purpose with a mind for home,
or the thinker intent on endings uncharted,
lost in a river fog on a still night

    I am unable to make a homily stick
    and fasten my thoughts, foundering, to it,
    unable to make a sighting certain enough

the river has neither course nor current;
the last point of the relative compass,
upstream/downstream, falls away; the duet
of waterfowl and waterfall, complimentary
virtuosi of distances untaken or taken
and forgotten, is joined to dissonance.

VI

Tonight, the Mare Tranquillitatis,
like a thumbprint on silver,
and oddly, like a street name
or an address, the Plain of Jars.

"This feather stirs . . ."

wind's wing across water,
something brushed aside,
the care taken, her eyes;
what we had imagined in
the trees, as though witnessed
at it and afterwards feared
so many things otherwise
common, the quickness
of small animals, birds,
dragonfly and cicada.

Quiet takes back her
folded fields. Elmshoot,
chokecherry and willow
clamor above shadowed
watermillions, the Leek-
green grass, buffaloberry,
"which strikes & profumes
the sensation," those busy
tides, treacherous sand—

how it swirls and gathers
where rivers join—
the Platte's due payment,
distant soil "with great
velocity roleing," as though
the high plains in visitation . . .
the bitter places, destinations
we already have names for,
all that is said of what
most surely awaits us,
wind and water, this green
tumult, its weathers.

Think of the clouds
as surfaces in time,
the river bank as
a banking of clouds,
that what is seen here
folding over itself
is a gathering of those
pasts we voyage into
and so watch it all
with practiced apprehension.
This peculiar edge of things
wears toward us at its
own pace, the scree
of distant mountains
configured now as leaves.

Marsh of Sleep, Sea of Crises,
Sea of Serenity, Lake of Dreams.

VII

Among the provisions they carried
across tidal drifts of sand
and wind drifts snared with weeds—

hemp-bound faggots dipped in pitch
and flat-bound sheaves of grain;
so the land was parceled first

in cross-stands raised on a salt
beach, each household counting its
remaining necessities, thus counting

the lands they were wedged into—
sweet soils beyond salt bogs
and stiff grasses. Rivers, trails

where Spanish armor rusted into
dark mud. What they had expected
was a magic, wholly accessible, devout

as daylight, gold the western sun
displayed, cities of gold, resplendent
in that holy fire. In a tangle of

purpose—dream and vision—there
were many caught in this soil, clutched
down among their metals, decaying.

VIII ("signs is *signs*, mine I tell you")

Time and time again, snake's
head rising to the doe's
udder, and her, fresh-killed,

hanging over the water
and no great distance from it.
I threw chunks and drove

this snake off Several times;
was so determined, I was
compelled to kill him. Peeled

Some bark to lay down on,
gathered wood to make fires,
Heard the party on shore.

So much always moving away.
Be quick about it! Fond
farewell, watery grasp. You

rest your head one evening
against the powdering sand,
say a few words, murmur

to the gathering dark—
umbruliata, the enshadowment,
trees' long slant, hillside

and what lies beyond, that
brightness faltering, as well.
Broad expanse of the river

turned to blood, red hue
drifting into gold or boiled
with rings, many-tinted as

an opal. Graceful, smooth
circles uncoil each syllable;
what was said to her, embossed

in gold, crept by me upon
in the waters: colors of departure—
sunset, the stars' terrible retreat.

Centered, now, by all that leaves
us behind, its red calibrations,
our lines of sight played like

taut strings, the present moment
trembles within other durations—
that clay, as though precisely

cut, its remnants swirling fire
at my feet, the galled leaf
flared from a bare stem,

snake's heads or flame dancing.
Light-play and murmur acquiesce
to image and parable, that tongue

flicking, our own incessant song,
how carefully the ship's pilot
steers past its raptures, dangers

the beauty shimmers here—
bluff reef, break, changing
channel and dissolving bar—

all that the castaway holds
dear, drifted . . . drifted
precipitate of his bewilderment.

IX

The sunlight on the water,
landfall shadows, treeline
edging down the slow current.

This is the land I made for you
by hand, what was touched once
then misremembered into words,

place where the soil slips out
from under its trees, where
stiff weeds fall like rapids.

It is the made emblem of time,
that only, nothing we have,
nothing we have ever held,

and it is only my arrogance
that calls it mine, this press
of clay on clay, this sluice

for cattlepens and sewers.
So, sunlight yellows on water;
treeforms blacken at dusk.

"Meanwhile the voice continues,"
or several voices, mine, yours,
those others that slide beneath us

among catfish and bullheads
angling in the slime, water voices
that suck the current in and pump it out,

gills that speak back waters the river's
long swirl threads to oblivion,
and her voice somewhere in the rocky

watershed, as yet unformed, thrilling,
who speaks in tongues so quickly, child
at the sunny edge of constant snow.

X (In and Out)

In came the doctor,
in came the nurse,
in came The Lady
with the alligator purse.

That moving window of rope,
the hazed shape that swings
boundaries or hazards.
                                    Once
he lived here, often taking
a morning walk or afternoon
stroll along this street.

Did you know her once,
    forgotten, The Lady?

Surgical implements and appliances
still-lived on the porcelain table,
the delicate tubes that feed and drain,
hang translucent curves, coaxial;
a flexible bedside straw angles from
a smudged waterglass like a cut stem.

She held her gloves in one hand,
the limp fingers spread like petals,
dark and wilted, above her fist;
beneath her dress, where her crossed

legs pressed tightest, she ground
nylon on nylon into another breath.

They count in song
or sing the alphabet,
adding syllables to match
the jostle of their step.
In verses some words
are merely breath;
silences
are sometimes spoken.

   Go in and out the window.

The rope's click on the pavement
springs the half-circle out of shape;
the projector loop stutters and
Pasolini dances:
Il mondo salvato dai ragazzini,
toe caught and falling through
the flickering hemp casement.

         "the descent beckons . . ."

She cranks the head up
and turns his face to the window—
late light sluiced past
chokecherry across occluded eyes;

the brown water threads its sludge;
the sprung branches of a fallen elm
trail curls of yellow scum, turning
as the catheter bends southward.

> "there warn't no home
> like a raft, after all."

Each spring the land spills back
with the receding floods, the slag
of the gray flats hooked with rubble,
stiff weeds strung with drying mud;
the river's harvest bobs in the dark current.

Her hair swings and jostles
the dance the mud encloses—
coagulated drops slowing the turns,
thick chokecherries bead the light.

> "At Malvern, the trees . . ."
> Thwaites, Jim, Buckeridge,
> Gutheridge, the fisherman,
> Lewis, the birdman;

the woman, expecting flight,
as she calls the river's slow turns;
the Lady, shifting in her chair,
pulling the strings of her beaded sack,
snapping the florentined, flowered clasp,

click, the recessional: song and dance.

Out went the doctor,
out went the nurse,
out went The Lady
with the alligator purse.

On "The Riversongs of Arion"

The Arion of this sequence is a contemporary who sets off on a trip down the Missouri River from Omaha and gets stuck just south of the city. On July 22, 1804, Lewis and Clark proceeded north from the mouth of the Platte River about ten miles and pitched a five-day camp, named, for Silas Goodrich's catch of July 24, White Catfish Camp. This Arion's diversions, complaints, and plaintive anthems while stranded opposite what he supposes is that campsite comprise the sequence.

I have relied heavily on Reuben Thwaites's *Original Journals of the Lewis and Clark Expedition* and on portions of his *Jesuit Relations* and *Early Western Travels*. The sequence also owes a debt to Paul Russell Cutright's *Lewis and Clark: Pioneering Naturalists* (University of Illinois Press). My debt to Henry Nash Smith is deepened here, as well.

Captain Clark was the most prolific diarist in the early stages of the journey, and I have often retained his peculiar spelling as a key-signature of his idiom. The notes that follow deal primarily with matters that grew familiar in the course of this sequence's journey but which are not commonly available.

    I "silver tankers": Offut Air Force Base is situated on the hills over the river near the site of the Lewis and Clark camp.

  III "The always restless . . .": from Conrad Aiken's poem "The Kid."

"Terminus": Both Thomas Hart Benton and Melville *(Clarel)* invoke the Roman god when discussing the end of American expansion at the Rockies.

"Lincoln County . . .": Billy the Kid distinguished himself in the Lincoln County Wars, though the gunslinger here is an amalgam which includes Billy, John Wesley Hardin, Wild Bill Hickok, and a smattering of movie cowboys. "two sixes to beat": the last words of John Wesley Hardin.

"a border roll": Hardin's favorite trick, in which sixguns extended in surrender were instantly flipped back into firing position.

  IV The confusion over Sacajawea's first association with the Lewis and Clark expedition has its source in movies and popular novels, which have often presented her as an Indian "maid" who joined the explorers near St. Louis.

   V Whether Lewis was murdered or committed suicide at Grinder's Stand, Tennessee, in October, 1809, is still a matter of speculation. At his death Lewis was governor of Louisiana Territory, enroute to Washington and then Philadelphia, where he was to have edited the *Journals*.

VIII "signs is . . .": Jim to Huck, *Huckleberry Finn* (Chapter "The Last").

The story of the snake and the doe is Captain Clark's (June 23 & 24, 1804).

umbruliata: Calabrian Italian for dusk, enshadowment.

"Broad expanse . . ." cf. Twain, *Life on the Mississippi* (Chapter 9).

   X *Il mondo salvato dai ragazzini* ("The world saved by the children"): Pier Paolo Pasolini.

Much of the identification between the river, death, and the past comes from Confucius. An example is quoted by Mao Tse-tung in his poem "Swimming":
    Here on the river the Master said:
    Dying—going into the past—is like a river flowing.

(Willis Barnstone, tr.)

TRACINGS

The women were divided between
regrets for the homes they had left
and fear of the deserts and savages
before them.

—Francis Parkman

nothing but this continent
intent on its dismay—
hands, etc. bandaged,
a torn petticoat fringed
with lace, roseate frozen
fingers, or elsewhere
feet wrapped in burlap
scuffing new snow

after the indigo of their tunics
seeps back into the soil
this spring, the several springs'
dulling thaw and incidental greenery

what marks they made were
harrowed out by those who settled,
so set themselves against the land

whether to keep the land
open to passage
or parcel it to the plow
Benton and Everett argued

"English tartars," some said,
white savages to plunder the trade,
"only farmer and tradesman stabilize"

his head raised slightly
the dying woodsman
views the open plains,

"flat water" squalls
spilling stiff grasses
into the small shade a stand
of scrub trees gives his end

"huge skulls and whitening
bones of buffalo
were scattered everywhere"

the Conestoga's canvas
straining to the wind,
the plow's first bite,
the first indenture
of the rutted road,
crossties set down,
oil, asphalt glittering
quartz aggregate to the sun

the harrow's bright discs
crumble the damp shine
of the new furrow,

the wind dulls and sifts
grassland into dust

two days in the storm cellar,
wet rags to their faces,
the slatted door impacted
with wet rags, dowery linens

strange light at the cyclone's
onset, a cupped brightness
edging banks of dark clouds,
fields darkening in lines
of gathering dust, section
on section spilling eastward,

a straw drilled through a tree,
a team of mules transported
forty miles intact

a dream of transport, Dorothy
soaring on the wind, becalmed
in still another summer, lost,
follows billboards and Burma Shave
into the city's ragged sprawl

Uptown or Lakeview, five
children in three rooms, A.D.C.,
weathers like unpainted wood,
stacked porches where her laundry

tatters with city grit, bars
haunted by banjo music

everybody talks of home
as though it were the sparkle
of an earlier dream, a glint
of rainwater in someone's hair,
names you can't remember,
old photographs gone brown
with age, a man and woman,
faces obscured by broad hats,
a bare tree beside them,
the bare distances empty
and faded into the sky

Oxus, Phasis, Palmyra—
Oz encased in glass,
"variegated with fields and meadows"
store window dioramas
display the life and manners
of high-rise glass apartments—
The El Dorado, Malibu East—
warm winters, cool summers
high above the city's noise

clouds move in facets
across their polished faces,
tipped red at sunset, presiding

over a close-set clutter
of flat, graveled roofs

graceful as mannequins
they are laughing into
the summer evening, women
bright as spring flowers,
in autumn's colors,
warmed and smiling,
they talk of love
before a dying fire

gray as she is, aging,
she fingers the pictures
of ladies' magazines,
fingers, as well, pictures
she brought from home

the red flowers on the floor
wear into black treads, black
dust comes in at her windows

his weapons arranged at his side,
the sun darkening his sight,
Cooper contrived his death
in alien spaces; Boone finished
his days on a crumbling porch
that fronted on the open West

REEVING

Tricks of the weather
or sleights of memory,
another Sunday empty
of touch, so clear
this January seems like May.

Impositions of dead fathers,
their remaining tyrannies—
the Dutch-German I never knew
panning for gold or harrowing
South Dakota into dust, quick
flashes of amethyst across
the blackened winepress
when late sunlight reaches
my grandfather's cellar,
hard spring of plowseat,
the dying gambler in black
coughing into his cards
or oiling the blue sheen
of his stub revolver.

More, certainly, than is needed,
these insistent returns—
as though the flat of Nebraska
were closing like a hand,
the rivers we have lingered by
spilling out through life-line
and love-line, the lines

of fortune and trade,
the slough of old soil.

Only the dust of hands,
season on season, what
gathers in the boot of
an empty silo or sifts
into the widening lines
of a rough-cut floor,
gathered back to haze
the city in, salt streaks
across dry pavements,
winnowings of a long winter.

AFTER-MILKING

(burden of that hyphenation,
what fulcrum for the quartered
moon on some dairy's calendar)

lay silent there, waiting speech,
the hay dust sifting down
through the rough-cut floor

call it cowstain, the must
that grows upon old wood
like lichen, blossoming with age

indefinite children, lost farms,
still the straw points caught
in your trousers itch and sting

and the gag of warm milk catches
just where the words begin, you
swallow it back and start all over

MATERIALS OF JUNE

Clear vials of cloudy
sputum on a windowsill,
the hand they said I saw
waving from a balcony,
that bony face of his
buoyed up in tufted satin.

Three times as many years,
they sprout among the peonies,
open in the froth of new flowers,
so many petals where the features
find themselves again, floating
as the insects do their work.

Hand like a bare stem waving
in a windowbox, fingers in
the thin spread of unleaved
branches, vague arms in shadow.
Overnight the dandelions
have coughed up their seeds.

They are spinning in the air
like phlegm in draining water
until the grass snags them still
or you suck them in with your breath;
they root down there, forked tubers
with hair-thin tubercles extended.

BLIND PEW

"nowhere to go, nothing to see"
we are all tired of the news,
wait each night for the end,
the newsman's cardiac arrest

"you might as well come quietly"
these days our consolation is
that we might be the last to go;
this is also a matter of rivers,

the man at the button going first,
dissolving into his pointed finger,
so much spring snow feeding a small
stream, stream to river, river to sea

too many clues, too much to remember,
an odd recitation we make or hear
set down as evidence, nothing in the way
of declaration, not a public statement,

but that someone, certainly childish,
ourselves in another guise, may act
on it, might set out for distant
places, dreaming of gold and silver

FIVE SONGS IN SEQUENCE

i

begins there
among hands,
as though by
accident
and wanders
by its own
turns, discovers
or lies still

ii

you thought it
had been designed,
proceeded by some
strategy, going
from left to right
and as usual
downward
in and among

iii

so many years,
the car creaks cold,
the movie I
want to neglect
tangles its own

bodies, heaps them
against surf,
landing-craft flap
open, they charge
through seawater
fountained with shells

iv

take it from there,
late spindrift of
old leaves, rollers
heave his shoulders,
his back arches
above flotsam

v

how is it we
always know who's
going to die,
how he will run
across the beach,
how the tracers
will rush to meet him
or speed along his
footprints splashing
sand, the one who bit
his lip, the other

who talked of home;
we stir in our clothing,
almost ready to be
afraid, slouch back
and breathe small passions
into an already
interrupted night

THE JUDY TRAVAILLO VARIATIONS

for Eugene Wildman

Of course the other one looks just like her,
but if you really know her, you can tell
the difference even at a distance.

I

There is always the other one
pushing a cart in the supermarket
or standing on a corner waiting
for you to make the obvious mistake,
begin, that is, a smile and catch
yourself halfway, leaving your face
just that much in disorder, no chance
to recover yourself or turn away.

The problem and the test, knowing her
enough—the eyes, perhaps, certainly
not just the hair which shifts and tangles
or the posture that is put on and primpt;
that dress she wore once, the other might
take by stealth or even bargain for,
the one making the other herself briefly
in exchange for certain favors, anonymity,
of course, and possibly her own confusion
somehow relieved, the other wearing it.

And no one, knowing the facts of the case,
would blame you, knowing the disorder

she settles in upon you, the choice
you sometimes make, wanting only choice,
and after all the retreat is expected—
who wouldn't, knowing what you know—
and is judged only when she, the other,
takes your absence as her success.

II

For three weeks
among high lucerne,
saw them grazing like
cattle in familiar meadows,
birds bobbing their heads,
prized mostly for their feathers.

Lunch at the Royal Albertinia,
the consommé springing to the spoon,
the tea thick with mint leaves.
On the veranda talk of a trek
north along the coast.
The natives, they say, have
their women in common,
covering their bodies
with warm red clay,
all their wives becoming,
as the clay dries to powder,
the one wife they can share.

Whitney says this mission
requires more soap than sermons.

III

The arms and legs of Chicago—
fingers that push hair back
from the face, pick clothes
away from wet skin, the face
relaxing as the first air in hours
is drawn in between and expelled,
grit darkening the creases of the neck,
grinding like pumice behind the knees.

Her back to you, swaying with the train,
fine hair clotted with sweat, hand
passing, occasionally, under it.

IV

A cut-out Eskimo in cardboard
spells it out in frost, COOL INSIDE,
icicles hanging from every letter.
In the darkness the chill settles
down on your neck like a wet cloth.

If he had an airplane or a car,
could trail white vapor into ice
clouds above the tangled streets
or glide like a landlord through
the city toward country-club cocktails

and summer evenings with Lizabeth Scott;
if he had not begun so badly, desiring
so much, not taking it all with boredom,
tossing his cufflinks onto the dresser
from a bedroom chair, dinner jacket
sprawled across the carpeted floor.

It is hot tonight, she says, turning,
offering her zipper to his hands.

V

Lost again, strayed from the picnic grounds,
they should have tied him to a tree.
Alone, his Indian companion or the dark-
eyed lady from the grocery store
gone back for supplies or help,
breechcloth or lace panties drift
down the sluggish stream; he fishes
it out with a branch, remembering
his devotion and her eyes when they parted.

NEWS NOTES, 1970

for John Matthias

i

and the bottles   rocks flew
Grant Park   the yachts still
lolling their slow dance of
masts and flying bridges
tear gas   a few gunshots
evening papers tally the costs
in police cars   fashionable windows
several injured   none dead
fear a new alliance beginning
"the brothers and the longhairs"
"mellow," one said   surprised

ii

music from a flat guitar
its neck angled across
his crotch like a gunbelt
right arm almost straight
music like the stone extended
reports through the microcircuit
concussion registers rock
against a head just turned
the tallied windows   cars
overturned and burning
a mellow swirl of bodies
breaks over the ear like music
fades out with evening

echoes only in newscasts
prolongs a traffic jam

iii

if we could name each part
pick through every archipelago
the city's wash contains
species that waddle
history through the streets
islands brush past us
their clatter gathers
volume   then subsides
the landscape dips and curves
notes for a full catalog
curl in the fire
new explosions contend
with old salvage   sludge
the air we crouch in
expecting martial music
beating through the drone

iv

for two weeks studying
a handspan of spruce
extrapolating glaciers
the silt this limestone
still imitates   breaking
into flat shelves   lines
the receding waters left

trees rooted in their faults
pine pitch fills the air
a cardinal flares in the brush
moving against its greenery
as water moves against stone
closing off this valley's
tumbling progress with
repeating crest   break-over
ebb   and sounding fall
as ice moved a millennium
as the earth moved   extruding
silt compacted into stone
as we move now   compacted
shouldering buildings into
place   hefting post and lintel
shouldering it all down
cities   valleys   plains
the intricate dance of greenery
we presumed the world at rest
tread into a widening slag

PINE TREES WITH CHILD

for Francesca

Waft, wave,
the pine fronds,
limestone where
lakewater curls over
and, sounding, falls
under spread branches,
green haze, blue eyes,
the child I hold up
into the sunlight
thinned and shifting,
nymph flies spinning by.

We begin to forget ourselves,
are almost casual; two jays
clatter blue wings upward,
three quick slaps, only
the widening ripple, perhaps
the dark body's single flash
as the fish falls back,
thus reasoned into place.
We can not help supposing.
Eyes wide, she turns,
head following just that
part of it, some span
of this day's moving.

FOUR POSTULATES

for Anselm Hollo

I

what is most valued,
the cherished things
any moment in Iowa
settles so carelessly
upon you—cat stickers,
a coded signal Home
Orange Juice is trucking by,
some morning or any day
when winter spring summer
and the poem begin again

II

who was it started laughing?
someone otherwise somber,
the Christmas lariateer
spinning double circles,
dancing through the lasso
at his side, bullwhipping
cigarettes from his lovely
assistant's scarlet mouth
every hour on the hour
next to the howling Santa Claus

III

would have thought other-
wise, conceded the point
at first argument; of course
there were mornings, the hills
went on to Cedar Rapids
and Davenport; in its own season
the corn's pollen stung another
hand; brown rivers paled with ice;
those were the truck washes we had
known before, the spit of gravel
from the humming wheels; the patient
customer of truck stops knows the best
of these returns, hulks them into
the dark of his coffee with rounded
shoulders and extended forearms

IV

it is the line of force or the vector
that sees us through our ambiguities,
diagram of rivers, path the semi
takes among its various winds, turn
the night makes at a neon sign, EATS,
locus of all points on the lasso's rim,
itself remembered; somehow each of us
knows the double twist of brittle fiber
that holds the line together, knows
the turns the rain takes, heaves
the long land rests against our feet

THE EDGE OF AUTUMN

The wind, a rustle of leaves
and brown hair fanned out, strand
by strand into blown leaves—

a light squall across littered
grass, a shimmering of leaves
and brown, blown hair.

A radio plays beneath a static
of leaves, dark maple, yellow elm—
Everytime we meet, everything is sweet,

and meeting, leaf-strewn, soft-
edged in a shelter of blown leaves,
her hair is drawn out by a soft wind,

and the radio plays the rhythm
of his hands sweetly across her
leaf-strewn back. From the black

plastic case, through dry leaves,
the news from Bien Hoa; it says,
one grieves at the thought of men

sprawled among rubble,
while the lovers, here,
cresting on a wave of leaves,

rubble at a season's edge,
strain to a memory of music,
the lasting rhythms of an insistent dance.

SHADOW PUPPETS

Against a room's neutrality
we cast the threat of words,

almost forgotten, how condition
and consequence gather whatever

shadows are available and gnarl,
ourselves gone strange at the edges:

a game for a child's bedtime,
the fox and the goose, their bright

geography, wingspread and mouth
gaping, a play of grace and need.

AFTER NERUDA

against blue moving
sea-blue, and against sky-blue,
some yellow flowers

October arrives

there with the sea's
great purpose,
its myth, its mission, its ferment,
the gold place
of a single yellow flower
sparkling
explodes over the sand,
and your eyes catch on the earth,
just a moment's rest
from the immense sea

we are dust, will always be

neither air, nor fire, nor water
but
earth
only earth
always
and perhaps
some yellow flowers

KING DRIVE

for Leon Forrest

Sometimes South Parkway
   slips into view,

steps out like
   Mississippi smoke

streams and curls
   away, talking its

music into cold fingers,
      this December

morning's blue jitneys
   catfishing by.

PRIMARY EXEGESIS

Nothing more than was
warranted by her song,
incautious morning,

occasional bits
we thought that day
could be gathered

up like bachelor
buttons, late spring
nosegay, nothing more.

In time you notice
the colors seeping
from the dahlias

staining the glass,
and the day darkens
there, and it will not

come clean, the whole
winter's diligence
at smaller things,

morning sunlight
caught by crystals
that grow in from

the edges of the glass
like plaited leaves,
so garlanded, chill blue

perfecting the air
to sharp sounds,
the wind and its metals.

She presses her hand
to it and the warm air
displays a moist corolla

that lingers and fades,
returns in slant light,
the first measure, some-

thing extended eventually
to fit my own hand,
its palm opening the day.

LUMEN

"Yearning and dying"
those old songs in
so many voices—

so warm today,
litter of sooted snow,
salt-streaked pavements,

some talk of seedlings
for spring planting,
windowbox fuchsia.

"No paroxysm, inward,"
this practical love
toward what unity?

Meister Eckhart, you
and your carolers
make very little

of the day's particles.
Those shafts of light
the soul is mirror to

churn with dust and lint,
are known by these only—
no radiance, *kein Wesen.*

The rich petals spread
downward purple and red,
flesh and vesture still.

SET/SORTS

Set

if she is where the paths stop
—James McMichael

Like accidents, surely,
such centers arrange
the land to themselves—
the folds of slanting
hills, wash of spring
rains, walkways you
only happen to take—

and yet the tread
resounds into centuries
of walking back from
apparent fields
or slips into ruts
of pilgrimage or trade.

She waits, unappointed,
at a place the land
designs for waiting,
an end of paths.

What will be called
the first map of this
occasion? perhaps
the floor she scuffs
impatient for your

return, furniture
her skirts brush past,
chrysanthemums beside
the gate, blossoms
black against sunset,
the cinder path you
grind with your heels,
remnants of plumb line
where old walls meet,
the known place where
skin moistens skin.

Sorts

I

In spaces where
touch begins, fails,
a quickening of air,

light churned round
in breaking water,
mounting waves,

that distant shore
our undercurrents
drift us toward, how

soon the sense fails
like crystal husking
its facets into some

dazzle without
weight or shape—
salt spray, this

dampness or all
yours, its wet
still settling,

that narrow wave
curling into you,
you ride as light

above its foam,
Cyprianna, yes, you
ride the afternoon.

II

In a close room,
smell of peat
from seedlings you

tend so carefully,
soft soil that
sucks its water in

with a deep breath
like air pulled
through teeth or

moist sighing,
the pale stems,
twin nymph-leaves

shaking as you
pass, gathering
your breath, mine,

together into what
freshness and our
familiar surprise.

III

Firepoints pressed into
our eyelids, the shapes
we give to darkness,

compounded of fire,
jostle like molecules,
already with us,

touch worn smooth
as a sacred stone—
so much devotion—

or sea-surge across
pebbles or river-run
gathering sweet soil;

so sleep begins,
slow wear under fire—
distant bird, beechen,

a shore, riding inward,
bluff-cut and canyon,
now a sudden geography.

IV

White water and stone,
time to speak, morning
chill against glass;

awake, some green
at a fixed distance,
a few steps from where

the dream churned itself
into air, restless foam;
said, good morning—

good morrow, some
space of the night
still damp between us.

V

Instants to our fingers,
years to the hand spread,
arms stretched toward that

vacancy, place the dream
once fully sustained,
reluctant pastoral.

117

VI

As though the music
fell about us, hazed
vistas, tender cinema;

grown old and weary,
past dying fall to Webern;
all said, something stops

in that landscape grown
full behind us, such
unseasonable snow—

the borders our turning
sets there, those lands
by our absence divided.

A HANGING SCREEN

"In warm sunlight jade
engenders smoke"; poetry,
like indigo mountain,
keeps its distance;

the light plays words
and figures, stone's
edge edged with air,
green haze growing.

Amused by butterflies,
Chuang Tsu dreaming,
the emperor's heart in
spring, thoroughly transformed.

Still, in pieces, the words
rest so much apart.
Risking my life I lean
on dangerous railings.

When the dream wakes
to its own particulars,
the strands scattered,
loose hair on muslin,

broken characters
the reeds make, unmake—
vague   no reason
bright   again   dark—

the sidewalk's fracturing,
damp willow twig
forked there as well
locust seedpods:

Autumn, then, and
gourd music, the wind—
indistinct   no-stop
break   again   join.

Drifting between narrow
bluffs, sharp bends
enclose us, deep
rain-cuts all around—

mountain pass, slant
sunlight and snow line,
the dream piazza
gilded into a high valley;

"haze, mist," Kuo Hsi
interrupted, sluice-
way wedged into
a mountain like a keel;

what was said by fire-
light, the bandit in
the yellow sombrero
laughing at the window.

Chill surprise of
Chinese apples, glitter
of the Pacific between
buildings—caught in

passing, an empty
rowboat or Russian sealer
riding at anchor, Magellan
full sail in dusty curtains,

casements groan like
taut rigging, bright
shore, the heat lines
full of spice, breadfruit

stretching to our hands;
a new nourishment, this
mission, or shaded rest—
Pitcairn, a century or more.

I wanted to make this poem
of silk, stretched tight
and polished, an ink wash
drifting ambiguous mountains,

words gathered like momentary
details, instances of wind
and water among loose foliage,
painting *au plein air;* that is

alive and painting a surface
of perpetual change, the eye's
return always at odds with
memory, however certain;

the wind's warp in the cloth,
pressing the brushstroke back
full of squalls, relaxing
the line out of reach.

AFTERNOONS

Quick passage into
memory and behind
only blank spaces,

blue stain on pink
litmus or merely
known so closely

something falls away
receding from touch,
caught in the air

your fingers move,
agile water-fly
padding the surface

of what is seen
even among these
defractions, bent

pencil or warps
of a flat eye,
the wide world circling.

OURSELVES

This gathering of chance,
each of us, a swirl of
occasions, flesh their
first coincidence, what

passes through us,
waiting some arrangement
of our smallest parts,
a clear space opened

into an eyepiece or a lens
and beyond, symmetry of planets,
not, finally, a geometry
spherical or plane, sweet

press of movement, place
where the space is
always closed, always opens,
eye to eye, each eye unseen;

what we brim up to each
other called vision, touch
moves so readily among,
something is passing through.

RETURN

I

The distance back is greater
each time we settle on the journey;

it is a game of chance, this play
of time against the lay of the land,

the hills stretched flat, wheatfields
spread thin, abrupt highway towns,

brief irregularities of line, sloped
now like telephone wires at the window.

II

How will it begin,
second by second,
the strum of a taut cord,
an accumulation swirling in,
late snowstorm drifting long
shapes, snow fences bellying
like sails to its weight,
or built up, day by day,
like the glow of a glaze painting,
the light coming back through
layered strokes as luster
and curve from the still-life's

expected oranges and bottles,
or raged up like silt and rubble
with spring floods.

III

We know so little of weight,
she said, since we've come
to believe in flight,
so casually, as though lift
could measure anything at all.
Go to the corner, watch your
shadow lengthen as you pass
the streetlight, edging into
the next darkness. You push
your own contingencies before
you, carry those distances, also.

INTERSTATE 80

The detail, of course
it quavers in our view,
like the verge we press

the highway toward,
edge of an expected
season, implied greenery,

water shimmering always
at the same distance,
ever retreating spring.

O my America! moist
hand at the wheel,
the present moment

flattened like an insect
on the windshield, traces
of color, bits of wing,

reminders of an ulterior
delicacy, the wind itself,
a quiet air transgressed.

ESTHÉTIQUE DU RÂLE

What we are confused by
is hardly less relevant
than what we know,
the examined assumptions

of our meanderings into
words ordered by rank and file,
tallied, etcetera, graduated,
the quick-step and the plod,

neither incidental, neither
wholly acceptable to those
anarchies of speech that bind
us to the days we mouth,

breath to unnumbered breath.
And yet the perfection of speech,
tyrannical dream, a fine sibilant
opening that white space just there,

as a single leaf defines a field of light
and light curls at the leaf's edge,
each, in turn, the other's hypothesis,
amused fingers amid amorous conversation,

how the tree veins itself to the touch.
It all goes on like an afternoon,

something past into which we propose
these other occasions, habitual landscape.

It is highly unlikely that the question
of touch itself will be resolved in our
lifetimes, the problem of the eye's
skittish focus, a simple unreliability

in objects each of us knows by heart,
each proliferating daily. What song?
"a single image," a lifetime played
among light and surface, on edge

and falls silent. Old *crystal acorn,*
what is there left to break away,
only the husk of clarity
and brightness alone unfurled.

Something is ending, as though
the weight of combinations,
the spread pigment we give
the universal gray—think of

the houses faceted yellow and red
into the simplest hills, another's
sense of fabric, bright arabesque,
the extended dialectic surfacing

a single guitar, insubstantial
as graphite to the touch, a casual
movement among flat particles, sheaf
of paper slipping just now from your hand.

They have taken to heaping dirt
in abandoned places, firing kitchen
matches, Buck Rogers fashion, at
their wives. Perhaps it was too much

to ask them to resolve our difficulties;
they seem unduly nervous and afraid.
Even the paint—how elegant it is!—
seems to want to fall away with each

passing semi-trailer truck. We know
how the day went, the guest list
of the party down the road, the Cadillac's
fish-tail and impact, have seen the lunge

slow-motion, chest pushed forward,
arms out, the head's brief hesitation,
bits of color settling with city dirt.
Somehow it matters more than its irony,

the fragile surface, commemorating chance.
It is only in isolate flecks, swift
and mutable, light finds its shape,
all that the form fails to exclude,

the almost unbearable clamor, every
gesture ambled among traffic, this day
or any other, talk settling in with the
portioned words, meant, I think, to be

a flower, a field of flowers, where
the wreckage seems oddly comfortable,
a seaside morning dew over bent metal
and blue Quaker ladies, *le dernier cri.*

THE SKY AT ASHLAND

How temptingly the landscape shines!
The air/ Breathes invitation. . . .

I

Dust–colored water, golden-
rod, the oil–spattered leaves
of broad roadside grasses

shimmer here. Each summer
the river wears itself away,
silt slake, uncertain rivulets,

or is it that the river itself
is wear, the endless cut of mud
and wet sand, an approximation

among cottonwoods of brown
water, thinly present and
foregone. The sky at Ashland

feathers white contrails
above sunflowers and grey silos.

II

Pollen-soft wings rehearse
the properties of light:
translucent loiterings
along the planes of sight.

. . . or shape the air
around us or lift this
brightness yellow flutter

by flutter into a shaped
diffraction, each broken
instance, flash of sunlight,

each quick facet in slow
water, quartz aggregate,
leaf, blade, flower, dances

now and in its own turn
bends, darkens or subsides.

III

Regret seems so much a part
of beauty, as waking to the dream
or love to its fretted absences.

Taste has hunger and hunger its own
forgetfulness. Bite hard and fast.
Only the aftertaste appalls, a grit

in the mouth, only fresh grit
can scrape away. The dandelion
she holds beneath her chin

offers its momentary blessing;
the scattered petals of another
wish slip into the contours

of her dress. She brushes them
aside like lint. Was the answer
hidden in the flower or what

was stripped away, the blighted
pistil or the bright debris?

IV

The meaning of the game
is neither odd nor even,
nor what is lost or found.

Numbers are only numbers,
a play of hands without touch.
She wanted the day to speak

to her of love, if only
in mute reflections, lowering
her face into the flowering light.

If the color hesitates one moment,
if the numbered petals leave one
petal imitating fire, something

flares like bass to feathered bait
or music to the memory of song.

V

Is this the ordinary blue
of a blue sky or some mutation
the Platte imposes upon it?

Is this moist soil the river's
residuum? The soft cottonwood
dappled marl, seed-fluff laid

on like white lead impasto
a condition of light?
Is the pale edge of the horizon

any more a function of point
of view than the bent shadow
that falls across spikeweeds

at your feet? Is the lambent
silo or sweet sorghum, foxtail
crown nodding or goldenrod

in full flower, pale silver-
rod and ragwort, shallow roots
like hunched otters surfacing

then slipping away, mixed
high plains grasses, dogbane
and star-petalled milkweed,

broomsedge and blue stem?
Are we able to do any more
than propose distances for this

brown meandering in a play of names?
If words extend themselves from place
to place, are their movements less

determined than the course of water
leveling itself or more diverse than
what sheathes it here like a plumed skin.

The arc of this moment and the next
are each, in turn, hypothetical.
The river is not a recurrent

instance of itself against the shore.
Every surface struggles to its end,
and end to end, they laze among us

steady and familiar. "Qualities
tend to perfect themselves."
The absolute moment of the river

is an object of desire, not merely
what we attend to, dreaming, or what
words shim so neatly into place.

VI

Forgiveness may or may not be given,
may or may not be sought or found.
If loneliness is the punishment

and loneliness is its sin,
then the sentence renews itself,
like a dry plain whose dusty wind

wears away the encroaching greenery.
The blue pallor of an empty sky
takes its color from unnumbered

incidents in the thinnest air.
The forked lightning beneath
a distant cloud branches from

an accumulation that has no
consequence but this quick
brightness and its aftermath.

Raindrops gather their weight
about the imperfections of the sky
the way the river draws itself

into the lands's cut and cuts away
in its own slow fall, reflecting
trees its moisture leaches outward

to sustain. This green love takes
to be its own redemption is the grace
of fault and accident, is the frayed

improbable circle of delight,
is the ring of the world, pale
haloed, imperturbable western sky.

LE JARDIN DE CLAUDE MONET

for Antonio Frasconi

It is not the hand
as much as the arm
that lifts the color
and sets it down, not
dexterity but grace.

Asleep among familiar
flowers, papers scattered,
white beard pillowing his face,
light dances like rainwater.
Under heavy lids, old eyes—
bridge, pond and steeple—keep time.

MT. VERNON GARDENS, 1978

Nothing goes on
like a river
and its brown

luster. Sometimes
it seems to slide
through us, not

in the blood,
strumming, but
in the under-

current of feeling
bulging like dense
water, moment to

moment, this dry
season, all these
years beneath our skin.

ON THE CONDITIONS OF PLACE

Loitered, you might say,
at the edges of the ceremony,
the golden colonnade, red
streaked yellow marble, cattle
so real they seemed to graze
upon the stone, the god
himself, flowing robes,
and Augustus talking again
of Actium, the honorable dead.

Love, things weigh on us,
certain occasions, the gods
in their auspicious moments,
men of state. Think of the crowd,
sun on the sun's bright
counterfeit, woe and wonder
shifting from point to point
like a flight of birds unfurling,
turning shut, then opening again.

I saw you once at the window,
twisting a strand of hair
around your finger, sunlight
curling inward to your touch,
poplars in the wind, white
underleaves like sea flowers,
lines of foam, bright wings
or sails in rough weather.
"Bid them all fly. Be gone."

Sometimes it seems that more
has been lost than ever remains,
that we live in a slow passing
among indecipherable signs.
Strangeness and charm, the numbered
particles of weight and light
spin out the patterns matter takes.
All that we know is consequence—
hand, hair, moist skin, leaf curl, the day.

As indistinct as water is in water,
places dissolve into places, words
among words, what is carried along,
names whose sense shapes our memory,
all that is said or might be said,
Palatine or Platte, a leaf, a stem,
a proper noun, a spit-curl of scum
that draws along a moving stream
the probable line of what is seen.

THE FAIR MAID OF RIBBLESDALE

for John Matthias

The stone, she thought,
the river and the sea,
the dale just past the treeline,

places you visit or recall
in conversation, somewhere
you plan to pass through

or avoid, the grass there,
flowers and sharp brambles,
the slant of one hill and then

another, how accidents like
these require a name and names,
in turn, accumulate a place,

and this place or that, as far
as you can see, a dale modestly
confirming itself with leaves

agitated or still, the circle we
make of what surrounds us, words,
like waves, defining the shore.

CONSOLATION

Whatever you want,
it was always there,
close at hand, even

when your fingers
falter above the song,
you hear it, the space

between, the way you lean
into the road, curve
a stand of dark trees

insists upon or sleep
requires. Desire is not
a special instance

but the ordinary slope
these intervals assume
an immediate consent

of mind or sense,
as simple and compelling
as light among the leaves

of stirring branches
or the nothing clutched tight
beneath a breaking wave.

SONGE VERT(E)

Lady, it is to be presumed.

As quick as anything,
hands, you say,
something to catch
hold of, momentum,
as in a blade cutting,

edges where the light
falls and multiplies.
The demands we make
of our pleasures
accumulate an

indebtedness, its
secrets emptied out.
At odds again,
and now we want more
than we have imagined.

This is the true song.
Notice how new leaves
fray moist branches.
Clarity is not
the tree's intent.

The crown of an elm
against a perfect sky,
the sky's perfection
measured by the tree
is a fact of distance.

MOTET

I

"At odds again,"
hands moving out
of the shadows.
And now, now
everything seems
definite, discrete,
fingers webbed
with sunlight
the tree lets through,
arms still in their
own time, circling,
catch up, catch
hold at the wrists,
like cell chains
in a watchcrystal
completing themselves.
Together again.
Shoulders, torso,
each one of us one,
once more. It is
hard to imagine
minutes just past.

II

"At odds again,"
hands moving against
the wind like loose
flapping things,
washcloths, words
long frayed with
careless use. You
wanted to say
it was beginning
to bother you,
beginning to wish,
wondering if thought
in broken light
could ever touch
itself, reassemble
itself. The King,
our promise, broken,
the sword we imagined
gone, hovers like
leafmold in the light.
Say it, then, the stain
of things remains.

III

"At odds again,"
elbow cupped into
wet leaves. After
love, there are
moments of clutter,
and no amount of
practice will teach
you to regard them
as anything more
than what you lean
against catching
its buried chill.
Keep your fancy
to yourself; facts
do not fade but are
momentarily obscured,
the work of hands,
touch and its out-
come, the absence
of touch, and distance,
the inevitable space
between, shapes all
our limitations.

IV

"At odds again,"
knee raised slightly,
sunlight and shade,
patchwork coverlet.
Bits and pieces,
the story of each
thing connected, end
to end, this instant
extended in every
direction. Not a
thing in space or
things in spaces or
spaces between what
space seems occupied
for this moment, the next.
We are not snowstorms
of ourselves, spindrift
and curl. The whorl
of action is a template
in time: the casual
shifting of leaves,
hands moving, the certain
flex of possibility.

MAUDE

What with one thing and another, angels
occur to her, and she talks of the heart,
that old advantage, place where the loose
pieces are folded and gather in.
It keeps the order she asks of the past.

"See here," she says, pulling at the skin
on the back of her hand, "how slow it is
finding its way, how slack the veins become.
You'll see how much the heart matters,
a quiet place inside, and angels tending it."

OUT WEST

Clara held her hand against the sky,
turning as though the arc of her palm
defined it. "Pale blue," she said. "A Gypsy
told me once my life-line seemed to stop
and start again. This is my second life
and my first sky." That was in Alliance,
Nebraska more than thirty years ago,
a span of high-cirrus clouds running
from southeast to northwest behind her,
the plains, as certain as anything,
lifting and falling, her hair like foam
breaking along a crest of prairie grass.
"I think whatever's here or anywhere,
remembering my other self in you."

APRIL SNOW: AN IMPROVISATION

Light tricks us sometimes,
like spring snowflakes, fingers
at the window, blue shadows,
as though winter imagined,
however briefly, could settle

in—the first split leaves
of the crabapple tree, a litter
of bud husks spindled in the wind,
shoulders hunched, coat tails
flapping, a lost bandana furled,

the grey sky's abrupt chill
or the feather line of white
crossing your path, the bitter
taste of snow caught in your
throat that will not cough out,

lake water like loose slate
shingles breaking. Years seem
all at once improbable, the rush
of sharp pieces against your face,
each one distinct, each cuts the same.

It is a shape that water takes
in air, this apprehension,
an inexhaustible fear the present
too often requires of us. Dreams
that shape us, shape more than

we imagine, quick as crystal,
an expression of structure,
angle on sharp angle, that is
not otherwise there, grows or does
not grow this fierce precision.

Suppose a hand soothed its way
across peach-colored linen,
fingerprints strumming the cross
hatch of fibers, as though some
music waited there or brushed

its soft transparent hair
until the skin beneath it chilled.
These might be the successions
of an afternoon, mere trails
of sense, distracted and invisible,

sure signs of nothing in particular
but going on, moment to moment.
The pieces of time are lost, tick
and whir, breath all but forgotten.
Songs slip in and out of place,

conversations, syllables occur
like accidents—spin the bottle.
The mouth that trembled, streetlight
and August haze, night bugs tapping
their lives away, snow white moths,

so many years ago, trembles still.
The trick of summer is going on
until too much accumulates and falls
out of the persistent brevity of sky.
April is the chance dampness takes

so seems unlikely whatever happens.
It is always the first time, catches
in your voice, the turn the sense takes,
something the sentence makes of itself.
Remember, she might have said, remember me.

SUCH SUMMERS

The choice perplexes.

1

Knee and twilight
after all. June
dampness, neon
along the way.
American elms.

2

There is no measure
for it but catches,
a nest of twigs
and loose grass,
bits of string
the rainwater
runoff leaves behind.

3

A snag in the river
curls, loops and spins
away, a branch, a stump,
the cross-piece of a broken
jetty, cloud-play, foam.

4

Brown light, the afternoon
sky like silt churning.

5

The crest of one hill
and another, section lines
like cottonwood quilting,
nothing we have not seen
before. "If it's all the same
to you," she says, turning
back, creekside loam
and bare arms reddening.

6

This watermark, like paper
torn against a table edge,
the yellow trace of something
seeping through wet clay.
We assume the landscape
explains these lines or must,
at least, contain them;
it is, in sum, their consequence:

a tree, a stand of trees,
the shadowed relief of hill
against receding hill.

7

One imposition after
another. What flutters
at the roadside as we pass,
edges the rearview mirror
like pictures wedged
into a looking-glass.

8

In August, the black seeds
roll like peppercorns
into your hand. Thirty-
five years, my father coughing
into the four-o'clocks.
If we return, it is
in search of accident.

CANTILENA

Buds, husks, leaves and flowers gone,
the ordinary city tree at dawn,
    the usual traffic,
    expected fumes,
    automatic music
    in darkened rooms,
dance step, disco, action-weather, jive—
top-of-the-charts, *Only the strong survive.*

VARIATIONS FOR A SUMMER EVENING

I have heard what the talkers were talking . . .

1

"Thank you and goodbye"
and now she turns, hair
asway, skirt furling,
the peonies, each one
of them a pink tangle,
sunlit quartz sidewalk.
Lester leaps in.

2

Flowering Cheyenne,
ladyfingers, white
blossoms, bees
and butterflies,
the skyline, pure
Chicago, this paper
cut-out of itself,
watertown solitaries,
a deuce-and-a-quarter
listing by.

3

The voice I hear
under the locust tree
in the courtyard,
so definite, the rush
of the El, box elder,
poplars stirring.
"All I want," she says,
"or anyone, for that
matter, is a chance
to show you what I mean."

4

Haze after haze,
the city and evening:
music seems implicit
in conditions perfected
years ago, gaiety,
the Venetian glass swirl
of warm gin over ice.
Dear saxophone, the breathy
instant before the sound
comes on like anything.

5

America, it's hardly worth
mentioning. These happy
accidents occur as they
occur, something the horn
ribbons out into moist
air and indigo. "To show
you what I mean," like
the lyric that stammers
inside the songs. *Embraceable
You,* never quite uttered,
assumed, like Max Roach,
an insistence that
sometimes comes to call.

6

Elm crowns above the scattered
rooflines, *my sweet,* the Smoke King,
so close you could hear him
fingering the keys, *embraceable*
valve pads opening and closing,
riding above the notes
and darkened leaves, breath flared
like steam against lacquered brass.
Sometimes this sadness is intolerable.

7

"All I want," the narrow leaves
like fossils stamped in anthracite,
"or anyone," ice cubes hissing
their breath away, an insistence
turning just where the light furls
round their sadness. "Thank you
and goodbye," *my sweet embraceable*
night air and its thickening
apprehension, "for that matter,
is a chance to show you what
I mean," *my sweet embraceable you.*

LUCY TO THE DRIVER

My sister Lotte lived
twenty years with a madman.
Flora thinks butterflies
have dreams they struggle
to remember. Anna sleeps
in fear of tornados and pale
strangers who know her name.
All my life I've wanted
to live in a warm place.

VARIATIONS ON STRYK'S BASHO

i

like the old oak,
Fuji, the Big Dipper,
autumn wind among cedars,
parched grass, voices

:or on account of these
recollections and their
brief certainties, sidle
across asphalt, loose

paper curled in its own
turning, not the wind
but the action of something
moving harshly against the air

ii

with leaves, bush-clover
start again, sweet song
sparkled with shells,
waves storming over, scaling

:and contrary to popular
opinion, very little matters,
the order of occasions, hand
just now raised, the riffle

in the skin, nerves strained
to the point of collapse,
desire and its intermittent
fondness for catastrophe

165

iii

my teeth grind, wildfire
hedge, sparrows, the gate,
all night years crest, I
grieve straw-clutching, crow

:grape-ivy along the screen,
reddening leaves, o yes things
not only move but alter,
and sometimes it seems

to our advantage to mistake
quick shimmer for change,
particle for cause, take
this dust to be a firmament

RATHER LIKE

Plays on and on,
old saint, this song,
the city at its

business, just
Saturday and the cut
out there so sharp,

as deliberate as
any type-face, locked
up, kisses the night

away, those other
edges, honed or blunt,
smack-dab. Something

breaks alright, some
lesser part and stumbles
home wounded and ashamed.

SUMS

I

Whatever bends or breaks
beyond repair, course
the night takes, hot
or cold, city figures,
windowsill and doorframe,

something to slip into
this terror, its lean
artisans, cutters, skinners,
the one who scrapes
a cleated heel along

the inner passage of
your ear; light breaks
sodium vapor or sunlight
faltering, the screamer
catching her breath.

II

A prism in gasoline on
standing water marks
the blue shift of
a gathering apprehension.
Everything is coming

nearer, closing in.
It hums through walls,
vibrates along a picture
wire, gear changes blocks
away, the night's engine.

"Alright," you say, "it'll
be alright," nothing more
than you expected
of this congestion,
a matter or probable

coincidence; all movement
implies collision:
raise the temperature,
increase the pressure,
and it multiplies.

Supposing, as well,
resonant frequencies,
diverse harmonies,
this wall, exactly twice
the length of a distant

axle, roof pitch an even
fraction of the highway,
picture wire held tight,
the fretted sidewalk
outside your window,

notches lamplight cuts
along the floor, bedframe,
the dark stairway's aching
banister, hand over hand
ascending your spine.

BORROWED MUSIC

for Ralph Mills

I

The water is blue and not turquoise,
nine and seven and one, the fates
scattered in pieces like words strewn
or characters without context, bits
of song, a black tree, the rock wall
angled against the sky, in the distance,
a figure in a great coat striding.

Under blue paler than heaven, serrations
of elm like toolwork on jade, its bright
curve defining in this light at least,
the prospect and consolation of evening.
First, the green line blackens, under-
leaf silver becomes shadow and blue sky
fails into vermillion like a vein opening.

Laurel bark sheathing the fugitive, thighs
grown rough and darkening, sinews tendrilled,
the first twig vibrating from her finger,
or found in the fault lines of the stone
itself as mere stone was cut away, stipule,
some quirk of vegetation caught in the slow
press of centuries she struggles into and from.

Until the mind jumps without building,
each step is its own politics, each word
its own forfeit; the song has already slipped
away like pale lips beneath distant waves.
It is only something we thought we heard,
like the cry of a young girl in blown branches
or the ring of the mallet along emerging limbs.

II

One thing, as relation to one thing—
numbers curl, and what should be a simple line
is a succession of waves. Between zero
and one, that space or the next, the slope begins,
advances and turns back, as though hearkening,
as though each point were its own occasion,
something to be remembered or acted upon.

Night against sea cliffs or a wooden bow-piece
lifting and falling beside a wet stone wall,
undulations of seaweed, backward glance,
the quarter-turn her hemline exaggerates,
grace note, grace note, how the implications
of ending fall forward, salt flake on grey sand,
a scattering of stiff grasses and broken shells.

III

White wind, white dew, here from the beginning,
moonlight on blown water. If you are certain,
begin again. *Pomegranate.* The clear air
above the streetlamps darkening the sky
toward lapis, the leaves of the sacred lilies
at my window pressing pale veins to the glass.
Nothing is certain without presumption.

Sea-foam reoccurs, kelp lines scrawled across
littered sand. How many years? he said, and over
what landscapes, drawn up, drawn out like fine wire,
drawn and turned? This is the song her breath might leave
if she were moving over a staff of waves,
moment to moment, as the night air moves its
bright molecules across the surface of your eye.

'Neath luna, then, all things in things conspire
figure and fancy toward song, as the dried grain
is lifted and thrown, as the light is caught
along the leeward edge of unbroken waves,
or these jade-green leaves tumble against glass.
Listen, listen, nothing here is closely held,
this dream or the next and their uncertainties.

IV

Out of dark and toward half-light, the mind's space
at the city's brightening margin, lakewater,
the sun—first, the highest antennas like tubes
of light, then the glass valances of skyscrapers,
rose-tinged, a knot of petals within a fist
of leaves. Improbable moment, like mountain
snow at first light and its opposing dawn.

And serenitas. Cars sweep, white sailboats loll,
the park's double row of indigenous trees
stirs and stirs. Behind a concrete portico,
the reconstructed spine of a mastodon
offers its airy permanence. All that was
or is, case after case of moths and butterflies,
edged flint, geodes opening like crystal seeds.

The waking world and its massive variety,
Brahms in bright coincidence, that liquid
silver trailing something overgrown, nearly
forgotten. Music. Pomegranate. Amethyst
in its dull husk all those centuries, scattered
vertebrae compressed to stone, the calloused hands
each tool implies, tropic air and figured wings.

One thing in relation to one thing, quickly,
or a sense of loss, as though the field you paused
in once, slow river slipping under exposed
roots and memory's dire complexities,
revolved around you. These bits of time spindle
and turn, each numbered shard coded to the arc
it shares with a probable amphora.

V

If there is nothing to animate this moment
I sit in—and nothing comes to mind—does it
all fail, the play of possibilities, count
down counted out, cecropia, viceroy,
pebble tools by the basket full, numbered bones
wired carefully into place, the sorted bins
of unassembled jars, vain antiquity?

Across the path a petunia riffles
in the wind, then everything around me—leaves
petals, branches—stirs like crazy. Sorrow is
a kind of order, loss a proposition
exaggerated by our faith in beginnings,
the sense we have that each of these surfaces
is a commemoration in time. In time

the play of traffic beside the lake subsides;
trees stiffen, then relax; before it falls,
the petunia manages a brief parody
of itself and its flowering. It is no
more emblematic than the lake's recurrent
surge or the palm print of a squall line, traffic,
conjecture, adroit leaves signing leaf veined mud.

CONSTRUCTIONS

A place you would be/familiar with
                    —Ken Smith

I

This is how the lines run,
like the uncovered beams
of an old porch, flaking,

and that is rainwater
thrashing the hollyhocks
against the west railing,

the smell of wet soil,
sweet memories, "the lost
Traveler's dream under the Hill."

II

Sorrow is commonplace,
morning and afternoon,
footsteps on the walk, just

one thing after another,
the song at the blind end
of the street—*ah love,*

the music goes round and round
like fingers tracing picked over
patterns in white chenille.

III

Lautréamont. Deciduous.
Left out. It might have
had its own shape,

the philodendron, or the space
the painted radiator gave
up to it. Now and then

these textures seem like bits
of time. Everything trembles,
hums a while and slips away.

IV

An iron bed in the front
parlor, white hair wisped
into its spoked headboard,

her fingers work all day
at one another, and sleep
comes and goes like the hem

of the blue lace curtain
fluttering in a small breeze
at the edge of the windowsill.

V

On the porcelain nightstand,
amber vials, her silver compact,
tortoise shell comb and brush,

a hand mirror, face down,
on its back, a spray of corn
flowers lacquered in;

visitors lean over her
like wishers dropping
coins into a well.

VI

Dark oval frames are best
for fading memories, faces
mourning barely holds onto,

pewter cheeks, brass eyes,
a knotted strip of palm
wedged into the glass, *ashes*

ashes, or a forked twig
pushed up into his hair,
sunshine and dancing long ago.

179

VII

Eyelet lace, mahogany,
the wallpaper pulling
at its seams, onion flowers,

the French blue wandering
veins—neck, wrists, hands,
eyelids, her skin thinning;

through the open doorway,
the vestibule light weeping in
like whey from knotted cheesecloth.

VIII

There are not enough leaves
to cover the girl stretched
out on the lawn or obscure

the dark branches of the tree.
This is the balancing act.
The boy marches back, basket

on his head, and shakes a few
curled specimens over her.
She laughs a little at being dead.

IX

Yellowjackets, the last
of the mud-daubers grazing
for spiders under the eaves,

white egg sacks everywhere,
the spent husks of night bugs,
black grit, old brush marks

chiseled in, here and there
the soft meal of old wood
hangs along loose webbing.

X

Cars pass, flick through
slots in the white fence;
over the roofs of the houses

flat clouds. Something always
intervenes, between this
and that, now and then,

like a curved glass bending
the room away from itself.
Torn paper, pieces blown away.

XI

We have talked for so long
about the limits of words,
all that they can not touch,

how the song fails us even
in its delight, things cut
short by what is said,

as though the hand could
be certain, the eye in its
lifelong fidget, exact.

XII

Think of it as a path,
the thread of common use.
Occasional footsteps gather

into a line like strands
of loose fiber, carded
and spun. These things

happen: the old woman waking,
the girl's shape left behind
in a scattering of leaves.

NOVEMBER OR ELSE: AN ODE

i

s'posing it was
pine needles
spinning at the corner,

barberry fire red
and sumac, box elder
yellow as anything;

s'posin it was
you with bare arms
suddenly and cheeks

all colored up,
sweater pulled off,
the sheer rustle

of everything
going to pieces
all at once

ii

Indian summer,
the jet stream pushed
way off to the north,

the slant sun bright
as August, leaf mold
stinging your tongue;

this is the measure
the harvested trees
exact from us, nerves

skipping across pavement
like flat stones over
still water, eyes

unsettled, unsettling
things, the dry
insubstantial fall,

spindrift and catches,
tines of the rake
pulling and pulling

its brushwork through
the softening grass,
the foreground shaded in

iii

steps and steps, you
want the warmth of it
with you always

the red, yellow,
burnt sienna tattooed
into the lines of your

hands, eyelids edged
with elm, a heart
of lilac on your sleeve;

there is a pink flush
fading into the centers
of late blooming chrysanthemums,

a second brightness
chilled over the dahlias'
last neon flowering

iv

old songs, old tunesmiths
weedle in and movie musicals
with hemlines riffling,

four hundred cleats to scar
the polished floor and fingers
feathering every kick and turn,

famas, each one of them, Julio,
and nothing to be done about it,
nothing to throw into the works

but ourselves full clamorous
and vain, kicking the leaves
that settle back into the dance,

shaking the stiffened branches
of the trees, so that the wind
might seem a choreography

v

s'posin I should fall
into the leaves and notch
my spine into a cold

they shelter from the sun;
s'posin we should run out
their circles like children

playing autumn without
consequence, as though the game
could be left behind at bedtime,

as though stirrings in the dark
were things we could imagine,
the brightness of the day,

the steep commotion of trees
and sky, chrome yellow, blue,
and tinctured argentine,

presiding, would all this
agitation delight and still
delight us in the light's decline;

old voices and old sorrows
still remain, old falterings
grown habitual with age;

forget them for a day at least,
they will come back, I promise,
with their fierce monochrome in tact

FOUR EXEMPLARY TEXTS

I

> *we live in the darkness in back of*
> *her   rising*
> —Robert Duncan, *Passages 23*

Living in a circle proposes
certain wonders to us; each day
the dark recedes before her face
and trails, like a long gown, behind her.

It is not a puzzle or a problem
to be solved; she is a pronoun
we offer to the day's brightness,
a face we remember against the shade,

bright with morning. Wake up,
she says, it's late, tomorrow
framed by columns of light, the spring-
loaded roller, a lintel above her hair.

This is the letter we share, two
strokes down and one across, initial
for the world, the light, the face
that waking always fashions there.

II

the little shrine of the Willow Maiden
in the midst of a willow shade
—Lu Yu, *Beginning Summer*

Villagers pass by like figures
on a screen. The river crosses
the foreground, mountains float
like smoke in the distance.

They pray for their crops, recite
a charm against locusts, confirm
the antiquity of the path they walk,
their place in the season's uncertainty.

The willow tree spills its narrow
leaves into a green shimmer, wind
eddies quick-silver at its edges,
its shade trembles with shadows.

Maiden, they say, the river is long;
the wide world is more than we can
imagine, ten thousand Li and shrine
after shrine. We wait for your blessing.

III

There were murmurs. Time defined them.
  —Basil Bunting, *Chomei at Toyama*

However we return, these shapes
precede us. Someone kept the house
in order, or something swept it away.
It is surprising in every detail,

the shape of the city that does not
remember itself but merely goes on
day after day, the land beneath it
shifting silt and marl, water table

rising and falling. Suppose the barn
remains, the afternoon light
across weathered shingles, the print
of the pumphouse in an untended yard,

remnants of a line of cottonwoods
noisy with blackbirds, a hint of sun-
struck mica in their flutterings, you and I
insisting we are what we were here before.

IV

Elegy, let down your hair!
—Ovid, *Amores*, III, 9

I wanted to tell you a dream
and give it back the sheer luster
of sleep, the way a leaf is held
in a moment of crystal light, how

places drift into places, times
shake free of time, the unexpected
spindrift of faces, afternoon's
quick shimmer across the incurling

surface of the night, morning,
the worn yard outside my window,
the prairie everything subsides to
lifting quackgrass and bluestem

against each footstep, what the angel
said, hammered out in goldenrod, play
tag, the wind scurrying dust at their
heels, flatwater plainsong, this laughter.

WAITING THERE

As others or ourselves
let's say—furtive, then,

inconsequent and sad—
or on the edge of thought,

perhaps, or into some
predictable meandering,

the outward accelerations
of water against its shore

dissipating into erosions,
cuts and counter-cuts,

remembered as landscape,
the convenient certainties

of an abandoned past.
Is it tree or treeline

or the massing of leaves
against the sky or color

freed from shadow or something
of color deepening against shade,

the sensible bluff that heaves
above the bluff's presumed

insensible marl? River,
again, always enclosed

by its own turnings, its
own turnings overgrown.

AUTUMN MORNING, 1989

Avianca, an explosive device,
the suitcase detonated

just off the runway,
fragments to be analyzed.

Gorbachev in pixels,
above the Vatican.

"Historic developments."
"Sweeping changes" promised.

"The resulting uncertainty
carries with it a measure

of risk." "Everyone is now
accounted for." An office

worker with a video camera.
Allegations that some

equipment may be faulty,
rain in south Florida

knocking at our door. Some
one's knocking at our door.

All at once history seems
workable. "Not in my life-

time," she says, her face
in full color, coloring

the grey, impervious East;
twenty years of graffiti,

its small, bright offerings
taken up and passed around.

Sweeping changes. The office
worker with a video camera

picks her way through rubble
once again; San Francisco

is falling, falling. At LAX
the suitcase in smithereens

across the tarmac, south
Florida jacaranda glisten.

No trace of plastique, then,
among the shredded underwear,

no message sent to Medalline.
"Not in my lifetime," she says,

the Square brimming with purpose,
videotape unspooled and passed around.

GIN MUSIC

You listen for a long time, half-listen, even,
and then one day something catches you, almost
off-guard, a little bit of sense to it, buoyed
up out of the familiarity of things.

I'm thinking of Bill Evans, in particular,
the way he sometimes hesitates as though the keys
are pressed part way down and then reluctantly
strike their notes. There seems to be a slight

breath there, if you know what I mean. Well listen
for it, it's there, like something you need to say
but don't really want to let it out, except
that you're already into it, so what can you do,

and besides, the person you're talking to, well,
she already knows what has to come next, just like
we know, listening, that it's going to go on
to the next part of the song. *My Foolish Heart*,

for example, there's almost a sigh, right
at the beginning and again each time he gets
to the center of it, a deep breath taken in
and expelled, and then the notes come on

like words you know you're going to have to pay
for in the long run. I could listen to that guy

forever; it's like me being played or you
or any of us, the part you don't quite remember,

how she waited just for a second for the words
to fall out the way they had to and how you
waited, your mouth already shaped into what
you were about to say, and here it is back again,

the ache of it. That's it, isn't it, the ache
that somehow gets lost, well not really lost
but detached from the plain facts of the story.
Then suddenly, it's back inside this piece

of music, a taste that seeps up from the bottom
of your mouth. So you put the record on
or you hum through it or you go off to some joint
just in case it comes out right, but mostly

you want to play it yourself, just once,
so that your fingers would be the ones
settling down on the keys, and it would be
your shoulders hunching, then pulling back

just as the flat of the keyboard softened
in your hands, and you would be caught there
between silence and music, and the music
would pull you along. And whatever you said

or did leaning toward sound would be jazz.
And the smoke would curl its faded indigo
over the black lacquer of the piano,
and the ice would clink clink in the dark,

and faces would half turn and turn back,
and the song would ease its way out into
the room like a root extending itself
into damp soil and take leaf and flower.

FIVE PROPER NOUNS

from Johannes Bobrowski

I *Ostra Brama*

Wherever rivers move
they move from place
to place, from far Ostra
downstream, and your eyes
among the reeds, moist hands.

If I said, all is lost,
losing sight of you or
clutched a handful of wet
sand into my fist until
it pressed back at me,

would this soft passage
take another shape, curl
and curl its ribboned
currents like hair into
a snarled castastrophe.

II *Novgorod*

The cloister and the cloister
bell, light after brief rain,
the evening coming on, river
in its own complacent luster.
How can such riches not cast

off a singular moment,
something to be placed here
like a jewel on dark velvet
or the bright ring the pike
leaves widening itself away.

III *Tschernigow*

As dance imposes itself
on the moth's bright circling
or hills enclose the town,
the question itself proposes
the sea swell and the voyager,

not as answers but as its
answer's properties. Only
the story strays outside its
own radius, the moment the shore,
however strange, is sighted,

and the ship is dismantled
from its crow's nest downward
and chopped madly into fuel
or its store of coal on fire,
going down in a hiss of steam.

IV *Kaunas*

Branches over the river,
leaf stains on the stone walk—
I know the steps, the slope,
this house, house after house
running down to the river.

And the faces, straight on,
then averted, my own glance
implicated in that sudden
turning away. When the grey
line of murderers walks

the path you take each day,
touching what you know by heart—
leaf, stone, and shingle—
the water's quick shimmering,
spins off into an early dark.

V *Pustoshka (1941)*

These plains run off the edge
of sight. Mountains we have
names for hold imaginary
distances in place. Wind
in the rafters, a chill

seeping up through the wooden
floor, cloudbank moving in.
Emptiness is a form of waiting;
good times and bad, you
keep your ear to the ground,

SEVEN PIECES FOR UNACCOMPANIED VOICE

for Charles Simic

I

like tapwater in your hand,
momentary and familiar,
the strains of an old song,
"dear heart," leaf rustle, the night's
hum humming against your ear,
pulse taps on the pillow keeping time

II

"a thistle across my way,"
a thistle's breadth, caught hold
there, greying, as though some
part of me turned on this
coincidence and everything
impeded itself, briefly,
then hurried along

III

nobody knows, nobody cares:
the lady at the streetlight
shrugs up into herself, moths
in their busy circles rise
into a chaff of nightbugs,
shudder, stop, shudder, baby doll
pumps on the concrete curb

IV

"and all the marks remain"

V

chalk lines in the rain,
the lines you scratched
on the sidewalk in brick,
grass stain, milkweed sap
across your pant leg, creases
in your hand, the threads
they stitch into your heart,
fortune and memory fading

VI

nobody knows how we keep
ourselves to ourselves,
the circles sadness spins,
bits and pieces of the night
suspended by whatever swirls
down into this old sediment

VII

"They strike the ear of night,"
he said, and the day's eyes
flinch, sharp heel on stone
or stone on stone, the legends
we make of what is lost
and what is still impending

TOUCHING THE GROUND
(Earth Day, 1990)

I

Nothing we know of seems
more certain than this,
the struggle of the leaf

against the bud, the first
pale heart of lilac, box
elder and locust tree

quickening, ailanthus,
the tree of heaven,
splitting the sidewalk

once again. Clouds rush
eastward, a chill rain
clamors off the prairie

and subsides, and it is April
everywhere, like a green
swell breaking into air.

II

This is the ring of roses,
this is the barefoot dance,
the first place of mystery

we offered to the gods,
the breathless circle
and the deep heart's core,

the earth's first green
wind-flexed into the light,
sea grass and sea anemone,

the melting edge of mountain
snow, soft rainforest humus,
an airborne orchid snared

in prairie grass, salt surge
through coral, the granite
fissure composted with pine.

III

Ashes, ashes and a burning
rain, half-lives in ground
water, the air made bitter

in a bitter trade—forest
sold, river entailed,
whale bartered for a plastic

grocery sack, molluscs scattered
like small change, birds
bargained for feathers,

prairies for asphalt, otters
for oil, ourselves for gasoline.
Ashes, ashes—the grit

that catches in our throats,
compounds we exchange
for the enzyme and the gene.

IV

All growth grows on what
has grown. The circle of water,
the circle of air, the great

circles of plant and soil,
the blue circumference of sky
converge in the green space

of a single leaf. Between
leaf vein and leaf's edge
the earth offers itself

and its long history, a green
coincidence balanced briefly
on the planet's stem, stipuled

to our fingers and our eyes.
It is neither wilderness nor park,
but ourselves we celebrate and save.

AS IN A POURTRACT

for Denise Levertov

1 Early lilacs

Husks gathered like
kelp lines, the walk
veined over with them,

vestigia beneath
a bright fringe
of new leaves.

2 Glory-of-the-snow

As blue as
anything,
star-petalled,

centers bright as
sea phosphors
and cold.

3 Grape hyacinth

Each morning,
this driveway
devotion for you,

Hyacinthus—fruit,
wine, blood and flower,
saying your name.

4 Scilla

"The name of your delights,"
velvet blue flower-head
turned downward, fine stem,

an ornamented letter,
inked in or stone-sway
in sea water and song.

AND SO

after Paul Desmond

You were saying, weren't you,
that the choice you make spins
a little like the foam the ice
cube leaves in your drink.
You were saying that choices,
that the lift of it—voices—
you were saying, sooner or later
everyone decides. Were you
singing just then or merely
humming along? The drift
of leaves, so many of them,
how they shape the air, Audrey.
The foam that curls against
your ankles, chill morning
leaves and blades of grass,
reed wet and trembling, tendons
your walking plays into view,
toes finely turned toward humus,
sky running among treeline,
the sheer sway of cloud furl
like music arching into song.

POCHADES

for Ed Colker

I

Across a narrow lake, cottonwood
clusters, leafshade and windshield

cinema, sun and sky spattering
the glass, and the movement beyond,

within—arms, clothing, insinuated
shoulders, quick as silver fins

beneath rocking brown water,
what is guessed at and held dear.

II

Out of heaviness where no mind moves
at all, the surface line of water,

its portable horizon. They say
it is sometimes necessary to get

your bearings as disorienting as
movement eventually becomes,

turn after quick turn, the sudden
landscape becoming accidental, strange.

III

An empty waterglass, winter light
at the south window, chalk marks

in ringlets descending, as though
the water had strummed itself away,

or played once, a string plucked
over white pine, the saw's teeth

drawn along the soft line there
and glass sectioned into bangles.

THE DARKER COLORS

for Rosemarie Waldrop

sit and spin, things
rush past you this
morning, all gone,

as though you hid
your face in your
hands and vanished,

so far away, the plains
rivers mountains swirl
light and color always,

but you've already said
so, more or less, and
the tidal shift of words,

nightlong the moon's
bidding, shadows you
inhale like memory,

the counter-stress, sun‐
light and color always.
as though you hid

rivers in your hands,
inhaled mountains plains
the deft continent, deep

forest umber, a cleft
in the sentence, night's
glacier and its moraine,

words inhaled like memory,
neither true or false,
the shift along the wetted

surface where mass warms
itself, day and night,
into its own long valley;

set ridge pole, then,
and square the corner;
plumb whatever rises

out of the floorplan
scuffed in prairie grass;
rest, rest a while; the words

you want to remember, face
buried in your hands, drift
with you and curl like smoke

THE FINALITY OF A POEM

(after Albert Cook)

All day, that
is forever,

they fall, leaves,
pine needles,

as blindly as
hours into hours

colliding,
and the chill

rain—what else
do you expect

of October?—
spilling from one

roof to another,
like words from

lips to lips, your
long incertain

say in all of this
unsure of where

the camera is
and how the light

is placed and what
it is that's ending.

"NOT THAT FAIR FIELD"

for Mac Hammond

There is a vertigo in every order
where the numbered pieces eddy in,
the fringe of trees, a single leaf
lifting and falling. Words stir
at their stems; eyelids stir in sleep.
We accumulate interiors, the dream
and its predictable durations,
frequency and stress, electrolytes
slipping away one by one, or brimming
like water above the rim of the glass.
Perhaps the world is not "not enough"
but too much, an assembling of
catastrophes, wave fall, leaf clatter,
the taut improbabilities of skin,
floodcrest, fingertips and eyelids,
heartbeat fluttering, the onset of song,
pomegranate and ink smudge bursting with seed.

FIGURES IN A LANDSCAPE

In the space between
highway and highway,
a parchment of wintering
grasses, the Luwian adjective
and the name of Troy.
It is not that these
pieces go together,
but that it falls this way,
the afternoon retreating.

I want to say each moment
is its own antiquity
or that each sighting
in this tangle of light
threads the denser stuff
of accident, and accident
sways with us here and there
through time, and what is near
as love to the heart bends,
curls and bends back again.

If I should call us both
by names that are not our own
but keep the familiar order,
some part of us would remain,
air and light and wall, you
and the steep city. This
privilege of voice is pure
substance. Between this hill
and any hill is conjury
and syntax, and this hill
this steep, an inclination
bearing substance into time.

FACTUM, CHANSONS, ETC.

for Gilbert Sorrentino

I

"In a name
language, in
addition to

names with
determined
meanings, such

as Prague,
names with
undetermined

meanings, such
as *a* and *b*, may
also be used."

II

The pin-cherry branches,
the leaves of the pin-cherry,
pin-cherries themselves.

III

Trolley wires cross
and recross the plaza,
until it seems

absorbed by them,
Prague in Pathé
black and white,

the remote excursions
of recent history,
a field of vision

in which *b* is *a*'s
inevitable foreground
or the camera's incidental

fixation, a point of focus,
perhaps, indicating aversion
or simple inattentiveness.

IV

Calendula falling into
the weight of their flowers,
the first of the small mums,

grape ivy and blue gentian,
mulberry stains, the dark
remnants of mulberries

in a mulberry shade, green
against green luster and chalk
white tracings of mulberry yeast,

the brief ferment briefly known,
drawn into the moist grains of
broken soil like watercolors

drawn into moistened paper,
the spreading, frayed bands
of color signifying hill-line

and bluff-fall, the long
consequences of wind and rain,
the jagged tumble of vegetation.

V

Shall we say
that in Cathay
these stains once

marked an indiscretion
and that the dew
on stockinged feet

was veined with
amethyst, that one
devotion and another

are interchangeable,
that like gardens
they teach us gardens

more precisely than
newsreels teach us
their plane geometries.

VI

If *a* is the city, gray
and somewhat out of focus,
and *b*, the sharp trolley lines,

or if the foreground
is scattered with mulberries
and pin-cherry is a tree

whose gnarled branches shine,
if the watercolor mentioned
in passing is undesignated

and the antiquated chinoiserie
purposefully skewed, the residue
of decaying fruit seems reliable,

the dew of silk, the leach
of paint or ink through paper
and crystal remnants, called flowers,

with calendula and chrysanthemum
as points of momentary reference
or medicinal flowers of sulphur

sprinkled into an open wound.
The street-fighting has subsided,
but the night air smells of cordite.

"Sing to me *auf Deutsch, meine Liebe*
of sorrows deeper than our own;
recite, in Czech, the names that we

are dying for, as the city grows
vaporous and insubstantial, shifting
from celluloid to shadow at our touch.

VII

In a name language, names
propose incessantly. Pin-
cherries always darken;

mulberries shade and fall;
the insinuations of flowers
or cities under siege proliferate,

and like the dew on ancient
stockings or *a* or *b*,
they have their own chronology.

VIII

Quick, then, before it slips away,
for what there is at hand demands
the more attention always. Impending

time insidious twists and turns
the course things take and take
upon themselves, and consequence

is always multiplied by consequence.
Indeterminant, the city of Prague
blooms easily in partial shade.

It might have been the Old Town Square
with its clockwork version of the stars,
the Belvedere or the Waldstein Garden,

a sunlit conjury of grape ivy,
whose small fruit never ripens but explodes,
dusting the ground with pale green ivy seeds,

the Plague Column on the embankment,
Seifert circling and recircling
the four Apostles seated and writing

above the fountain at its base, empty
now and littered with cigarette butts,
and the sun only hesitantly shines,

and grief merges with apprehension.
"Be quiet city, until a hand at night
pulls down a blind and hides the target."

IX

There are no silkworms here
except that the mulberry tree
or 'mulberry' contains them

the way an address contains
a house we might visit there,
reading backwards to find our way,

and the gauze stocking, the dew,
the pin-cherry with bright, veined leaves
and bitter fruit, blue gentian,

called ague-weed or gall-of-the-earth,
a country simple for the plague,
the Plague Column and its apostacy.

X

Someone moves behind
a tattered shade,
or the moving shade

adjusts his shadow.
Sight-lines falter
among trolley wires

like silk moving
across stone in
unsteady light.

From the Fortress Wall
to the edge of Olšany,
a trail of quick-lime,

old hands sorting through
forbidden flowers, the cries
of gentian, mum and henbane.

"I have tasted a little honey,
and, behold! for this I die."
Bittersweet and black mulleins,

please, and a pinch of
belladonna for the pain.
Nightshade and ballistic

phosphors, the Julian Fields
flash their tracer-lined palms
too quickly to be read.

"Lie quiet city," Lie quiet.
Something moves among the jade
green leaves, some filament

drawn from mulberry to mulberry,
some moist, habitual line where
skin recalls its life in skin.